G000019906

MAD, SAD, DYSFUNCTIONAL DAD

STEPHEN GILLATT

Mad, sad, dysfunctional dad

Published by The Conrad Press in the United Kingdom 2019

Tel: +44(0)1227 472 874
www.theconradpress.com
info@theconradpress.com

ISBN 978-1-911546-55-9

Copyright © Stephen Gillatt, 2019

The moral right of Stephen Gillatt to be identified as author of this work has been asserted in accordance with the Copyright, Designs and Patents Act 1988.

All rights reserved.

Typesetting and Cover Design by:
Charlotte Mouncey, www.bookstyle.co.uk

The Conrad Press logo was designed by Maria Priestley.

Printed and bound in Great Britain
by Clays Ltd, Elcograf S.p.A.

To my amazing wife and beautiful children –
without you I'd be nothing.
I love you all so much x

To my mum and dad – thank you for putting up with me,
guiding me, for everything x

This is for everyone; fathers, people who have or are living
with mental illness, and the amazing partners, family,
friends and professionals who love and support us.
Just, thank you x

CONTENTS

What is the problem you are seeking help with and why did you consider seeking help at this time?

- Depression, social anxiety, low self-esteem (no self-esteem), self-loathing, guilt and inferiority complex, paranoia, mania/mood swings, irrational thoughts, difficulty making eye contact, insomnia. Thoughts of self-harm.

How does it make you feel emotionally?

- A failure as a husband, father, brother and son, trapped, like I have no direction in life, I have a job but not a career, I'm not actually good at anything. Very dark moods, disgusted with myself and every aspect of my life, that my wife would be better off without me, and that I don't deserve my life, and should end it.

- Physically my sleeping and eating are both very erratic. I don't shave often or use mirrors, I suffer from very bad tension heads – like it's pressed in a vice, my weight and mood yo-yo's. As well as short term memory blackouts and am very short tempered.

How do you currently cope?

- Walks, herbal drops, time away from social situations, not using mirrors, fishing when I can, speaking to family and friends, sometimes alcohol, sometimes to very excessive levels.

What goes through your mind at the time? (E.g. thoughts, images, worries)

- The oblivion of death, losing my wife and daughters, them being better off when I'm dead. Losing my job/home, my children getting terminal illnesses, being rubbish at my job, drifting through life, having no skill set. That few people care or understand me, that my wife deserves someone better, that she'll eventually leave me, and that I'll deserve it. And if my life just needs ending.

How long have you been feeling this way?

- I said six years. But my suicide attempt was ten years ago - before I left my first wife. I think I've had trust issues with women all my life. And that has flooded into the rest of my relationships, and the rest of my life.

Are you currently, or have you in the past, been involved with other services or talking therapies (e.g. social services, community mental health team, private counselling)

- Yes, I was referred to FCS talking therapies last July. This time I self-referred

How much alcohol do you usually drink in a week? What is your drinking pattern? (E.g. only in the evening, frequency of drinking etc.)

- Either a Friday or Saturday night, after the girls are in bed – the amount can vary, to a glass of port, to bottles of wine, or large amounts of rum. Although until recently I'd cut down quite a lot. And was losing weight.

Do you use recreational drugs? If so what and how often?

- No, I haven't for many years.

In order to know you are getting better, what would you like to be doing in the next couple of months that you are not able to do at the moment because of your difficulties?

- Enjoying my family time rather than feeling disconnected and pre-occupied, looking for a new career, fishing, not always worrying about my career, life, failure. Not feeling I must justify everything I do every second of every day. Feeling less manic, worried, paranoid and restless.

Have you been experiencing any thoughts of harming yourself or plans to end your life?

- I did make one attempt about ten years ago. I washed down a lot of Paracetamol and Ibuprofen with a litre of vodka. And when I passed out, honestly didn't think I'd wake up. I was prepared not to.
- About six months ago I put a large knife into my gut in the kitchen. I stopped when the pain got very bad, although I did draw blood.
- A couple of months ago while walking to work I saw an empty beer bottle on a wall. I wondered what it would feel like if I broke the bottle and rammed it in my throat and if it would kill me. I crossed the road, picked it up for maybe a minute, then put it down and carried on walking.

Have you been experiencing any thoughts of harming any other person?

- No.

This is the second time I've gone into therapy in fourteen months...

But let's start from the beginning...

INTRODUCTION

I'd known for a long time I wasn't well – years, decades. But I was too stubborn, and proud, to admit it. I also didn't understand what was wrong. But I didn't want to, or couldn't, look into myself for answers. I went months and months, never using mirrors. I just used to make jokes. Saying I didn't care about how my hair looked, or if my shirt was ironed. But it went deeper than that. I didn't *want* to look at myself in the mirror. And face my demons…

Why would I? I'd always been a lover of people and parties. First there, last to leave. Full of life - I'd do anything for anyone. But things, and people, are rarely what, or who they seem.

Attack is the best form of defence, right? If you're always taking an interest in others, it deflects the spotlight from you. I wanted to make people happy. To create memories and moments people would remember. It gets to the stage you almost become an enigma. People lose touch with the real you. And more importantly, you lose touch with the real you.

My name is Stephen Roger (hate it, because people ridiculed me for years, no idea why) Gillatt and I was born on March 6, 1979. In many ways I'm one of the luckiest men in the world. I grew up in a loving family home. I'm the eldest of three siblings. I have two younger sisters.

I have few early childhood memories. I was average, academically. I wasted a grammar school education - leaving after my GCSE exams, most of which I attended high on weed…

I remember turning up to at least one without even a pen. Outstanding! Despite my buffoonery, I still managed to pass eight of them.

When I was seventeen I went to live in France as part of my college catering course. Up until I went to therapy, I blamed my family for making me come home. I loved it there. I wasn't bothered about England. Or the people I'd left behind. Until a few years ago I never really felt I had any roots.

After dropping out of university I did loads of bar work. I've worked in most pubs in my town. Fired from some and carried out of others. When I was young my neighbour was my best friend. Back then we played in their garden. As we got older we both moved. And it was, and still is, fishing and beer. One Christmas Eve we were on a mission. A group of us had been drinking all day. It was snowy and icy underfoot. We left the boozer near my house hammered and he went for an impromptu piggy back. I collapsed under his weight and went face first into the road. The result you ask? He dumped me on my doorstep and rang the bell. My dad helped me up the stairs. I had a blended Christmas dinner.

My dad still calls me Oliver Reed.

I worked in catering for many years. But quit that. The hours were horrendous. After travelling in South America, I started working for a small consultancy firm. I was there for five or six years. During which time I met, married, and separated from my first wife. I also travelled on my own to the 2005 Champions League final in Istanbul, via Bulgaria - a truly epic trip.

Then in May 2009 I met my beautiful, current wife. I was doing the walk of shame through town one Saturday morning.

And I bumped in to my sister and her friend, who I couldn't take my eyes off. I arranged to meet them later in the day. I couldn't stop thinking about her. And when we met up later that day we clicked; there was electricity and chemistry. And we've been together ever since. She's the most amazing, beautiful, strong, caring woman I've ever met. My mates always said I was, and still am, punching above my weight... I can't argue...

We were married on April 4, 2012 at a private local beach in Negril, Jamaica. Called Half Moon Beach, owned by a lovely couple who treated us like family. It's one of the most beautiful places on earth and I've been lucky to travel a bit. They created an experience we'll never forget. To them, and our wedding planner, we will be forever grateful. And we love you xx

On January 6, 2014, our first beautiful daughter was born. Those first few moments in the delivery room are simply indescribable. Becoming a dad is the most amazing honour. And by the end of this book I'll be a dad for the second time.

At times I felt and still feel, so desperately alone. Even when surrounded by people who love me. Hated myself because I felt nothing I did was good enough. Countless sleepless nights - loathing myself because I couldn't provide what I wanted to for my family - wracked with guilt that I was letting my dad down. Along with everyone else.

So, the suicidal thoughts and attempt. You must be wondering... Don't feel uncomfortable or guilty. That's the point of this whole thing – to provoke a thought; a response; or an uncomfortable, but perhaps important realisation, empathy or connection. It's something I'll share in more detail later. All I'll say is, I frequently think about how much better off people would be if I wasn't around. Something I think about? What do you think?

And I absolutely guarantee there are countless men living with this burden every day. Some talk about it. Some drink and or take drugs. Some exercise. Some are violent. And some only find solace by ending it all. The thought of these men suffering in silence ties my stomach in knots. It breaks my fucking heart. It's the main reason I never give up.

I've lost friends and family members to mental illness. This year we said goodbye to one of our old friends. He was a good man, a caring, gentle soul. He was also a young man. It was so sad. It's a vile illness. If you've started reading this and any of it strikes a chord, there is help. I promise... But you must be ready to accept it. Worried what people will think? Who cares? And are those people worth wasting time and energy on anyway? Me? I say bollocks to them. The only person who can truly look after you is you. I'm six foot three and over nineteen stone. Frame like a rugby player. It means nothing. Mental illness can consume anyone.

Standing in the delivery room holding my daughter for the very first time changed my life forever. In my opinion the greatest privilege anyone can experience. But even at that stage, I wasn't ready to admit how unwell I was. I've always battled with feeling selfish.

For me, the hardest thing about mental health has been accepting I had a problem. Admitting it to people around me; then asking for help. It might sound simple. That's utter nonsense. It's unimaginably, excruciatingly hard - so painful. A man admitting he's weak, vulnerable, emotional, scared? You may as well go out with the lads and drink Shandy... We're geezers! This doesn't happen to us does it?

14

So, here's the thing. I'm going to share the next year of my life with you - Managing mental health; and fatherhood. Trying to be a good husband; provider, son, brother and friend; living with body dysmorphia and co-dependency disorder. Insomnia; and the problems I've faced with addiction. Attending and accepting therapy. And money – somewhere in the bible it says money is the root of all evil. I'm not religious at all. Not my bag. But there has never been a truer word spoken. Think about the role it's played, and still playing, in your life? How it's affected you, and your relationships? So, here's to the next year of my life - mental health and fatherhood. No lies - no running away. No hiding – no secrets - total commitment - total fulfilment - full tilt.

ONE. THE EDGE

THURSDAY 15 DECEMBER
8.16PM

We now have a routine. I take my daughter to bed, read her a story, and give her a huge cuddle before lights out. She's three in January - and my greatest achievement. She melts my heart. Every. Single. Night.

The house falls silent. But it's still chaos. Like my state of mind. In the house, there are clothes and toys everywhere. In my mind, it's thoughts and scenarios. Will my nan live until after Christmas? Will I be able to pay her the money back before she gets too poorly to realise? How long will it be until my mum starts to get better? It's been months since her sister died. But her eyes are still filled with grief and sadness. And then there are the irrational thoughts about my current wife having a miscarriage and me cancer. (For about a year before I met my wife I'd convinced myself I had AIDS). I don't know where these thoughts are coming from. She's totally healthy. But they won't go away.

I've finally eaten. But I'm restless. My mortgage is taking an age to complete. And the thought of having to wait until after Christmas is making me ill. How can I face not being able to buy my beautiful wife and daughter a present? The scathing and self-loathing are starting to weigh me down; to encroach on every thought, every interaction. I feel a total failure… Why didn't I get it done sooner? Why don't things ever go smoothly? Why can't I save money? Why can't I provide for my family?

People say how proud they are of my daughter. And what a good dad I've been. She's the light of my life. But sometimes that means nothing. If you've been in this place, you know what it's like. You compare yourself against impossible visions of what you think you should be. It's a totally distorted view of reality. But to me it's fair and logical.

When I'm at work I feel guilty I'm not helping my wife more. She's now eight months pregnant - and utterly stunning - the most incredible mum and wife. And every day I fall more in love with her. But as she gets less mobile, the more pressure I put on myself. And when I'm at home, I feel I should be out earning more money, and looking after my daughter. It's impossible. I want to solve everyone's problems but can't even solve my own. I feel like a failure.

I went out for a lads' night at the weekend - boxing and beer at my good mate's gaff. All evening I felt like I was on the outside looking in. He knew I wasn't right. Sometimes I feel more alone in a room full of people than when I'm on my own at the fishing lake listening to the gentle ripple of the water rolling over the bank. Scary isn't it? My mind is starting to race.

The house is preparing for Christmas. But it couldn't be further from my mind. My wife sleeps in our bed. I sleep on the sofa. I say it's because I don't want to wake her if my daughter wakes in the night and I need to get up - lies. I don't remember the last time I slept well. I can't face the thought of lying in bed unable to sleep, staring into the darkness. But everyone has so much going on. That's why I haven't talked about it.

So near, but so far

Sitting in a room
Lots of close old friends
Feeling so lonely
When will it end?

I'm hiding with booze
Rum at the ready
Over-sized shots
Keeping me steady,

All the way home
Feeling like shit
Rum from the bottle
Providing the hit,

I don't know the time
Stumbling black,
My soul and the sky
Everything black

Rubbish night. But I need to write. I've told a couple of my friends my mental health isn't right. And they've given me sensible advice. One thing I've tried to do more in the last year is listen to people and take advice.

Sounds utter nonsense? But think, honestly. How often do you genuinely listen to people and take their advice? And why is that? Not wanting to admit you're wrong? And that you need help - especially for men. We don't talk about our feelings, do we? Nah, we don't need to…. It's nothing a few beers down the pub and a blow out with the lads won't solve.

Wrong…

It's my wife's last day at work today - a watershed moment. Our lives are going to change again very soon, and I can't wait. But I hope things get easier for her. She's been struggling. And it breaks my heart I can't do more. Even though I'm not sure I can. There's the irrationality again. I want to gouge my eyes out into a pint glass.

8.07PM

Been feeling manic today - I was worried about my foot, which has been hurting for a week. For a while I had it in my head I had a blood clot. That's not the slightest bit irrational is it?

I was furious earlier - I was told my mortgage wouldn't be completed before Christmas. The self-loathing flooded back. The man of the house not being able to provide at Christmas…

I felt like a shambolic failure. Had to cancel a Council Tax payment to give me some breathing space - and no, of course I didn't tell my wife. Why would I want to feel even more of a useless failure?

My mind often races at this time of the day. There's a bottle of rum in the cupboard - nectar of the Gods. The way I'm feeling I thought I'd have one. Settle me down. But I'm unsure how far I'd get through the bottle before I stop… (I'm still not taking anything for my head yet - ignoring the advice).

SATURDAY 17 DECEMBER
8.13PM

A long way…. Not sober.

I gave my wife a break and took my daughter to visit my parents. They played with her. I had a couple of glasses of wine. Did I feel guilty? Yes and no. More yes. Did I enjoy it? Yes and no. It took the edge off. That's it.

This afternoon we went to a Christmas party at my mother-in-law's house. It was lovely. Her family are. I sincerely mean it. But I felt myself getting uptight and stressed. I can't handle having lots of planned consecutive social commitments. I get claustrophobic and detached. It drives my wife nuts. I can see why. But I can't help it.

My wife's in bed. I'm drinking Desperados. My daughter is restless… I need to go and settle her down. She's not happy; but still amazing.

She seems to have settled…

The rum *will* be out soon. Drinking alone to relax - frowned upon isn't it? By whom exactly…? Judgemental twats and nosy bastards… A couple of hours on a Saturday night; is my time. When I look back on my life drinking alone has been intrinsically linked to immense pain. When I was seventeen I lived in France. After several months I separated from the lady I was living with. A week later she started screwing one of my 'friends'. Who openly talked about it in front of me - for two weeks I sat on the beach near my hotel drinking wine and Pernod. Only leaving to swim, sleep or buy more booze, and occasionally work. I'm still scarred.

Alco-hole

People take drugs to try and fill holes,
The only effects are the pain that it dulls

Everyone knows that the pain ebbs away,
But floods back when you wake the very next day

The hangover booms, the realisation looms,
That booze won't solve problems, anytime soon.

If ever

Years on I moved to be close to my then girlfriend after we travelled in South America. Then she dumped me. For a month afterwards - every night - on the way home I bought three bottles of wine. And drank them on my own; often not eating.

I've been in some dark and scary places - feeling worthless and undeserving of life. That's also when my gambling was at its most ferocious.

I've been through a lot.

But who hasn't?

SUNDAY DECEMBER 18 (MY SISTER'S BIRTHDAY)
7.49PM

Woke up stinking of rum...

My mental health has improved slightly. I'm still not taking any medication. I also haven't told my wife about my latest 'lapse'. Who am I kidding? She can tell. I shouldn't be lying to her anyway.

Think we all needed to chill out today. Our eldest has been her usual self. Fiery; fun and full of energy. I'm exhausted. But it's been a better day. Apart from the fact I'm totally skint. I'm trying to be philosophical. But being skint is hugely emasculating. And I'm sure loads of men feel the same. Whether we ever admit it is a whole different issue.

I told one of my close friends about my plans to write a book. I had to pick someone who'd keep it a secret and give me honest critique. He said he thought it would be cathartic. At this stage he's wrong. It's challenging. It's brutal. It's uncomfortable.

Still haven't bought my wife any Christmas presents. (It's shameful. I couldn't look my dad in the eyes when I told him). I need a fishing trip. Some time away. I know, selfish bastard.

MONDAY 19 DECEMBER
6.30AM

The recurring dreams have started again - the one where I get shot dead. This time I was followed to work but escaped. During the day my office was bugged and secured. When I came back from lunch three blokes in camo gear and balaclavas filled me with bullets as I walked across the car park. I woke bolt upright. After a few minutes I fell asleep, straight back into the same dream. I was looking at myself dead on the floor. I woke up immediately. And decided going back to sleep again wasn't worth it. That was about 4.00am.

I've done some reading into the meaning of dreams - apparently guns signify a fight for survival. And can relate to lifestyle, social status or career. How serious your fight is represented by how many people are shooting you. Urban location and gang elements mean the person experiencing the dream is likely to be overwhelmed, overworked and feeling weaker against the majority. In their real-life urban areas represent something man-made. Like a fight for financial survival or financial or social status.

When I was mentoring young, vulnerable people I used to say to them *Don't focus on things you're unable to change*. But I can't do it myself.

My daughter was awesome at gym class. Not even three, but a proper miracle. She's growing up so fast. And utterly amazing on a trampoline!

(My over-riding memory of the sport was going to outdoor trampolines on a local beach. Thinking I was the business, I jumped too high and lost my balance. I came down between two of the industrial outer springs, badly posting myself. I almost cried and filled my pants simultaneously. My old friend - we did everything together back then - nearly wet himself).

My wife has done an amazing job raising my daughter. I've pitched in when I could. They are bright, beautiful, feisty and independent ladies - which is why I love them both so much. My wife's back is getting worse. She's glowing with pregnancy but struggling with mobility. At least she's finally had her hair done. It's been driving her mad for weeks. I couldn't even pay for it. The self-loathing is indescribable. I wish I could shred my arm skin.

Thinking about starting my meds again. Not sure if I'm ready to become a dad again. It should be easier this time. But three years ago, all this was bottled up. I was a different person. Worries about my wife, money, mum, nan and Christmas aren't going away. But I'm managing them.

Payday tomorrow...

8.50PM –
TERROR IN BERLIN

Newswires are reporting a lorry has been deliberately driven into a Christmas market in Berlin. It's so sad. I hope London is terrorism free on New Years' Eve. My parents will be there.

TUESDAY 21 DECEMBER
10.30PM

It's been reported twelve people died in Berlin. It's so sad.

I decided to go fishing. There's a beautiful lake near my house. It's a crisp winter day. All I can hear are birds singing and the occasional car hum past. It's glorious. I'm here to escape.

The last day and a half all I've done is housework and dad duties. (This morning I wanted to get as much done as possible before I left. My wife's having some of the mums round for food and a play date for my daughter). Yes, it's my role. But I'd be less tired if I'd been working this week. I don't resent either of them. But I get worked up if I don't get any 'me' time....

Calling me selfish? I can't argue. If you're thinking *Well your wife probably doesn't have me time.* You're right. But I can't help it. I give absolutely everything at work and at home for my family. But the fact is I'm a fragile, caring, incredibly sensitive (nay, paranoid), overly-thoughtful person. The result is I get strung out. And this is possibly why I have such frequent ups and downs. Today I'm down. I'm wracked with self-doubt and loathing. I feel dirty.

When I was in session my therapist advised me to be more selfish. Her angle was if I couldn't look after myself and be healthy, I wouldn't be able to be the person I want to be both in and out of work. Stick with me. I'm going back to my sessions. Hopefully it'll give you an insight into what it's like. Or what it could be like for you. Make your own judgements. Form your own opinions about me and the sessions. If you're sitting comfortably, you might not be for much longer. But we're in this together, right?

It was a perfect storm of things that tipped me over the edge. My work environment was horrible. The re-mortgage was a mess. My daughter wasn't sleeping through the night. (Not her fault). Neither was I. Nor was I eating right. Looking back; there was another defining moment. My whole life I've been an obsessive Liverpool fan. But at that point I'd stopped watching games. I felt empty, emotionless.

I hate the term counselling. It makes people sound weak. That's utter garbage. We're strong, intelligent people, searching to unearth and resolve our problems. Many of which are not our fault. That's why I prefer the term therapy.

Anyway, I chose therapy. The mind-altering drugs petrified me. Mood stabilisers were suggested. Basically, they numb your neuro receptors and nerve endings. So instead of feeling the highs and lows, you feel nothing. There are varying levels of mental illness - many far worse than mine. And these drugs unquestionably help people; and save lives. Everyone's different. You need to do what is right for you. And not think about anyone else. I suppose what I'd like is to be able to help men, and everyone, identify their problems earlier. And not be afraid to admit and talk about them; that it's okay - and that people *will* listen. So, they can get help early. Early intervention - it must surely save lives.

I'll be honest. I didn't know what to expect. But it was far more uncomfortable that I ever imagined - the silences; the beginning. They were filled with my feelings. No self-worth or self-esteem. Feeling a failure; feeling inadequate. Hating myself for not meeting my own standards as a husband or father. Not good enough for the people around me. Not good enough for life – loneliness, guilt, paranoia, self-loathing and suicide.

Paranoia is a persistent, irrational feeling that people are out to get you, or of constantly being watched or listened to. The three main types of paranoia are paranoid personality disorder, delusional (paranoid) disorder and paranoid schizophrenia. The aim of treatment is to reduce paranoid symptoms, and improve the ability to function (Source: Netdoctor website)

My dad is my hero. I struggled until I finally came to terms with the fact, I'd never be half the man he is. My impossible standards again...

Over the next two months. I changed many of these feeling and perceptions. My route was: identify a feeling. Find out where it came from. Break it down. Unpick parts I had no control over. And break the emotional connection. Then deal with the other parts. And most of all try to think and believe I was a good person. That I made a difference to people's lives - that I deserved life.

That was possibly the hardest part. There was an eye-opening moment. A moment I realised so many of my problems were generated by events that were not my fault. But I was still carrying that guilt. It was at the end of the fifth session

I think... I cried. Not out of desperation; but relief. I'm still not fixed. But I like myself a bit more than I did. And for me that's massive. My friends and family I did tell did so much for me, without doing anything. Listening is a skill; an art. And feeling people are listening to you. Rather than checking their phones every two minutes; gives people a feeling of self-worth. That we matter, that people care.

I now have a couple of herbal medicines. Self-medication means I feel in control. And that's crucial.

It took me three years of very bad mental health to finally admit I needed help. Nobody knew how desperately poorly I was - or how I was wrestling with life. Why would they? It's not their problem! Wrong. That attitude nearly ended me. Now I try to be more open about how I feel. There's no other way around it - the alternatives? I try not to think about them anymore.

For a lot of my grammar school education I wasn't a nice person; a bit of a bully. I took the piss out of people - for no real reason. Give me that time again? That's the last thing I'd do. I hope I didn't hurt those people badly. But you know what? I took a lot myself. Maybe it was payback. I certainly had a weight complex. The piss-taking was relentless. For many years I laughed it off. But I was crying inside. I felt like no woman would ever want to be with me. I suppose that's why I drank so much. My mates were hitting on girls. I was hitting bottles. Maybe the last four years is karma. I probably deserve it. I don't want pity. It's just how I feel.

School's out; emotions in

I spent my school youth,
Hiding from the truth

I had no hope
Escaped through dope

From the outside I looked fine
All sunshine, no rain,

But it was only hiding,
My indescribable pain

The times I've thought about ending it? Firstly, was standing on the edge of a cliff when I was living in France. Second time was in my bed at my parents' house – knife bent into my throat. The third, and closest, was when I was sitting in my previous marital home with a litre of vodka; and all manner of pills.

These situations carried different emotions.

In my bed I was angry. I don't think I had serious intentions; but who knows. I was angry with myself for getting wasted again - and embarrassing my parents AGAIN - so much shame and self-hate. As soon as I drew blood I stopped. I didn't run downstairs. I just waited for the flow to stop.

The other two... I was calm; ready. In France, I was a mixed-up kid who'd had his heart smashed to pieces - at that moment life meant nothing to me. I only walked away from the edge because my parents were due to visit the next day. I couldn't handle the thought of them finding me. Had they not been on their way? Who knows? But as I walked away I felt guilty. That I'd not gone through with it. I couldn't even do that properly. I was a total failure.

In the house with the pills - I thought; I either leave via the door, or a body-bag. I washed loads of pills down with a litre of vodka. I cried for ages; as I was passing out I was thinking back over my life. I was ready. A little while later I woke up pissed; pills everywhere. I chucked up, painted the toilet. Then I tidied up and sprayed air-freshener and stumbled out the door before my (then) wife came back the next day. I've just recently started writing poetry. Some is very dark. Here's one about one of the only times I was serious about ending it all.

The edge

Pills and a bottle, covering the table,
Shuddering and sobbing, completely unstable,
It was dark in the sky, pitch black in my soul,
Decades of pain now taking its toll,

The bottle was empty, my vision so blurry,
As I talked to myself, the words were so slurry,
Drugs in my throat, on my jeans and the floor,
My body was broken, my emotions so raw,

I hated myself and so often I'd said,
Who'd really care, if they found me dead?
My eyes got so heavy, started to drop,
I'd make my decision, no time to stop,

My body was heavy, my muscles so loose,
Drugs and pills working; no need for a noose,
As my body shut down, I recounted my days,
My eyes closed shut through a blurry haze...

Amazed I woke up; with bad double vision,
Counted my blessings about my decision,
Had to move on, to try and rebuild,
Despite being broken, had to be strong willed,

The crossroad was there, so much to fear,
No-one was told, all those I hold dear,

Now it's time to be honest, cards on the table,
I can handle the questions, now I'm more stable.

I'm ready

5.00PM

I've still not bought a single Christmas present. I'm a disgrace...

WEDNESDAY 21 DECEMBER
8.02PM

Work was a waste of time. No motivation or focus.

When I hear people talking about other people behind their backs I always wonder (and worry) what they say about me.... It's the paranoia and self-doubt again. I think that's why I generally keep my distance. Sad isn't it? I did talk to people about my problems when I returned to work. But mainly so people couldn't gossip about me. And I wouldn't get paranoid.

The minute my shift ended I bolted. It doesn't feel like Christmas. I'm worried about my dad. My nan had a call from the hospital. (She's going back Friday to discuss the results of her MRI scan). His dad, my grandad, only passed away three years ago. And now he's faced with his mum having cancer. It tears me up seeing my dad like this. And knowing there's nothing I can do to make it better. Just keeping my fingers crossed. We've been to the cemetery enough this year.

Sometimes life is a prick.

My grandad was a kind, wise, gentle, hilarious man. For years I sat on the floor by his chair listening to stories about the mischief he and his brother used to get up to. He used to take me to visit his family in The Midlands. And I still remember visiting his mum in a nursing home there. When I got a bit older, the three of us (Dad, Grandad and me) used to go to a local pub for a beer on Saturday lunchtimes. They were some of the happiest times of my life. Memories are so important. I'm dreading Friday.

Christmas shopping in the city tomorrow will be nice. The market will be pretty. The atmosphere should hopefully make me feel more festive. I don't remember the last time me and my wife spent some time alone together.

I'm struggling. Money is a constant worry. It doesn't feel like there's any light at the end of the tunnel. I look like I'm ageing daily. My wife's getting bigger and bigger. Baby is kicking loads. I should be happier.

Should…

FRIDAY 23 DECEMBER
10.55PM

How do I sum up the last two days? Heavy… Lovely… Family orientated - a maelstrom. Good, bad, ugly. I'm wondering where things will go from here. A lot of it isn't going to be good. Ever been in a car crash? It's the point time slows to the point of almost stopping. And your life elapses frame by frame.

We had a lovely meal out today with my mother-in-law. She's a lovely lady… Strong, opinionated and decisive… Honest; generous, caring and sincere - undeniably where my wife gets it from.

From the first day we met, my mother-in-law has always been honest with me. And protective of my wife (her only daughter), which is totally understandable. She gave one chance

33

to prove myself - which I was truly grateful for. I rarely make promises. But I still remember the first day we met properly. I'd only been with my wife a few weeks, and we went to her mum's for lunch. I was welcomed with opened arms. Something I've never forgotten. I shared a ridiculously boozy trifle with her dad, (what a man by the way.) When a year later I asked for permission to marry her daughter? She told me that I would only ever make one mistake. But I'm sure she could see how much I loved my wife; even then - so far...? No mistakes.

My rock, my love my everything

Some people say the trouble and strife,
Me? Simply my darling wife

We met one morning, both walking in town,
I chatted her up, she gave me a frown

Later that night we met in a bar,
The most stunning woman in there by far

A beautiful bombshell, she lit up the room,
I knew that I had to be her groom

So loving, so strong, devoted and humble,
And picks me up every time I stumble

No matter how bad my head has been,
She's supported, loved and stood by me

She is simply a wonderful mummy and wife,
And I hope that she'll be with me for the rest of my life

It's Christmas Eve tomorrow (an hour). The house feels Christmassy (thanks to my wife). I've bought her a diamond eternity ring. She deserves something sparkly more than anyone on the planet. I love her so much. I'm all in. I just hope she feels the same way about me... I never take anything for granted. Not for one minute of one day.

Had a pain in my foot for about ten days. Forced to go to the doctor today; vitals and blood tests came back clear. Can't get an x-ray for a week. I'll look like a muppet if I've just trod on something.

The mortgage should be completed by mid-January. So, I'll be able to pay nan back by the end of January. Then some of the money anxiety will be over.

I'm worried about my dad.

Thirty-five days and counting...

CHRISTMAS EVE
6.12PM

It's been busy. We're finally done but I've wrapped no presents. That'll be later - with a large glass of Desperados.

I bought my wife another last-minute gift; a silver bracelet with birthstones hanging from it. It has one for our new arrival. Still no name confirmed.

Nan had her results, they're bad. She's going for a bone marrow transplant on Thursday. Dad said the last time she had the procedure it nearly killed her. We went there today to drop off Christmas presents. Not sure she's strong enough to have the treatment. It's heart-breaking.

My daughter is so excited about Christmas. She's put her food out for Santa. And her stocking over her bedpost - just my parents for breakfast tomorrow.

I've decided not to take any meds until at least after Christmas.

CHRISTMAS DAY
4.50AM

I hope you're blessed with a family like mine. And that you're happy. We've all got so much going on. It's time to appreciate what we've got.

Happy Christmas x

BOXING DAY
5.00PM

The last day and a half have been joyful, crazy chaos. Christmas breakfast was awesome. My parents brought some lovely port… That certainly put some zip into it! My wife looked at me and said, '*It's a bit early isn't it*'. My answer was short, but polite!

I don't think my daughter has stayed in one place for more than a millisecond. It's the first year she's properly understood and enjoyed Christmas. The living room is full of presents; and her beaming, beautiful smile.

My wife's been under the weather. And very emotional

(which is totally understandable). She really needs me now. It's time to be strong. But I'm not looking forward to going back to work. Not sure why. I haven't been right for a week or so… The dark clouds, my mind is heavy.

She loved her bracelet. I finally did something right for a change.

She's started putting her hospital bag together.

TUESDAY 27 DECEMBER
8.42PM

I'm burning up. The window is wide open, but my face is on fire. Due to time off for a bad chest infection and mental health problems I can't have any more time off sick.

WEDNESDAY 28 DECEMBER
4.20AM

I can't sleep. I feel awful. Not in a good place. Good morning world. No, fuck off world.

6.50PM

I came home early. My daughter accidentally kicked my wife in the stomach. She's fine. But I wanted to be at home with her. I'm physically and emotionally exhausted… There's no opportunity to re-charge. I'm running on empty.

Stories of Gazza are in the papers again - a magnetic human being with an addictive personality. And co-dependency disorder - according to his books. I suffer from both, but on a much less destructive scale. I'm able to manage my demons most of the time. What an amazing man.... I genuinely hope he's okay.

For a few years I had a problem with fruit machines. Although I never admitted it I'm sure people close to me knew I was in trouble. I kicked that addiction by going to GA. Under my own steam too. I was in my early twenties and broken - it took me three months. Now when I see people in boozers hunched over the things? I feel so sorry for them. I know what that loneliness and emptiness feels like. Pint glass in one hand, pound coins in the other. I wish I could help them.

My nan goes in for her bone marrow transplant/sample tomorrow. Her chemo is due to start around my wife's due date. My heart is breaking; it's just not fair. My nan's such a sweet lady. She doesn't deserve this. Nobody deserves cancer.

THURSDAY 29 DECEMBER
8.12PM

Work was awful. And like always, when you're clock watching, time drags.... My wife had a better day which was a relief; as the last few days have aggravated my irrational anxiety. I'm knackered. And my fuse is short. Came straight home and started cleaning... Only took a break to put our eldest to bed.

Social anxiety disorder or social phobia

Social anxiety disorder, also called social phobia, is a long-lasting and overwhelming fear of social situations. It's a common problem that usually starts during the teenage years. For some people it gets better as they get older, although for many it doesn't go away on its own. It can be very distressing and have a big impact on your life, but there are ways to help you deal with it. (source: NHS website)

My dad said my nan came through the bone marrow okay. I still feel sick.

Ready (Head) set Go

A glaze in my eyes as the shift begins
A foamy headset that cover my ears,
Interest so low, it grazes my shins
Feels like a place of wasted years

Hour by hour my shoulders slump
Clock watching down to every break,
So many biscuits, my stomach plump
Comfort eating a rookie mistake,

So many nice people I chose to ignore
My head says it's easier being this way,
I'm sure I'd be happier if I talked more
But it's not how I've chosen to get through my day,

The end of the shift, I spring out of my chair
When my headset's removed, a dent in my hair,
Head for the door, like I've been given the sack
But I'm not that lucky, tomorrow I'm back

My day off......

1. Made everyone eggs for breakfast
2. Got our eldest dressed and ready to be collected by Nanny Purple Hair and Naughty Grandad (My daughter's nicknames for my mum and dad)
3. Cleaned kitchen surfaces
4. Emptied and bleached bins
5. Hoovered and mopped bottom floor
6. Stripped and changed the beds
7. Hoovered rest of house
8. Cleaned and bleached all three bathrooms
9. Tidied all bedrooms
10. Put all washing away
11. Folded clothes on clothes horse
12. Helped make dinner.

And all before lunchtime.

If you've ever been in this situation (a small child and one on the way) you'll empathise. If not, this could well be a window into your future. If so, good luck. I'm not going to sugar coat it. Why would I? Rewarding? Unquestionably... Is it stressful? What do you think...?

9.00PM

My daughter spent all day with my mum and dad. She came back tired, into a tired house. We're all frayed and need proper rest. So many of you will know what this is like.

NEW YEARS' EVE
7.41PM

My wife had a bad night - our baby was moving around loads. It's a total miracle - and so humbling. I know many people who have either had to go through IVF (expensive and stressful) or experienced miscarriages (I can't imagine how painful that must be). I feel so lucky to be in this position.

An up and down year.

- We've had death in our family. And still cancer is hanging around like a horrible twat. My auntie was my mum's oldest sister. They were so close. She seemed to pass in the blink of an eye. I remember sitting by her bedside at her home. The day before she died. Holding her hand. Talking to her. It was so sad. She was a beautiful woman.

- My old friend passed away. A beautiful soul. RIP mate. We miss you so much.

- I finally admitted how bad my mental health was. The hardest thing was telling my friends and family. And the person I hurt the most was my wife. Why? Because I didn't do anything sooner. Often been a short-tempered twat. And distant too. It put a huge strain on our relationship.

And she was pregnant! So selfish. Now I look back. It was shameful.

- I got a full-time position in a new department at work. I had to interview while I was still signed off. One of the hardest things I have ever done.
- My wife fell pregnant for the second time.
- Another of my old friends got a cancer all clear. He'll make an amazing dad one day.

I'm having a glass of champers and very rare beef ribs. It's a little different to barn and house parties we used to have! Memories of being so hammered I could not climb bunk bed stairs to win my prize of a bottle of whisky. Dancing with my coat inside-out and stumbling home as the sun rose. Happy times…

What do you want next year? Personally, I just want my family and friends to remain happy and in good health. For my wife to have a complication-free birth. And our new baby to be born healthy. Oh, and for the mortgage to be completed.

I'd like to thank everyone over the last year who has helped me, listened to me, advised me, ignored me, put up with me, laughed with me, cried with me and loved me. The biggest thank you, of course, goes to my wife. I love you from the bottom of my heart. You are the most amazing woman I have ever met. You're so much more together than me. And take everything in your stride. If our daughter grows up to be half the woman you are, she could rule the world. After a very tough year I'm looking forward to 2017 and feeling more positive.

I sincerely hope you got what you wanted. And if you read this until the end, you'll find out if I do.

Chin x

TWO. MY FIRST MIRACLE

NEW YEARS' DAY
8.47PM

I need to start exercising again. Ever looked in the mirror and thought 'I look hideous?' That's where I am. The challenge will be finding the time once I'm back at work. As soon as we get home we have to do housework and loads else to do. Some people say, 'Just make time'. Not a clue.

MONDAY 2 JANUARY
7.48PM

My daughter had a rubbish night. At least she didn't wake my wife. But I had to go back to bed when she got up.

I'm pretty much out of my 'lapse'. But it lasted longer than I realised. When you're not feeling good; you lose all concept of time. (When my gambling was its most fierce money had no meaning either. I gambled my tuition and hall fees and dropped out of that course. I wasn't ready for a paper round. Let alone a journalism degree. Guess when I finished paying back my student loan? Last week).

We need to be more self-aware. We can't let things slide again…

I need to be quicker on the meds - and stop being so destructively stubborn. I know I will sometimes need help. So why deny it? Admittance and acceptance are still a struggle. Sounding familiar…?

Less than four weeks until our due date. But before that, our daughter's birthday is Friday.

TUESDAY 3 JANUARY
8.48PM

My wife had to go to the doctor again… This time she's been given antibiotics. And had a blood sugar test. I hope our baby comes quickly.

I'm so tired. And beginning to worry about how we'll (and I'll) cope. I barely have enough hours in a day as it is. I make jokes about it. But there are serious undertones. I'm scared. I don't care if it sounds wet. It's fact.

WEDNESDAY 4 JANUARY
6.40AM

Dad's birthday.

My mind is buzzing. I'm not in control of my thoughts. Are you? Is anyone? Too much pinging round in my head… Like a bag of popcorn heating up in a microwave – Pop, pop, pop.

It's my dad's birthday. How many more will he have? How many more will I have? Will he get to see his third grandchild grow up? Will I be around to raise my children? I don't know why it's consuming me today. I struggle to deal with the concept of total oblivion. Maybe you do to? I know I'm not alone.

Our family is having a terrible run health wise. Why? It's not fair is it? We've all been here - feeling totally helpless as life and time roll on. No more than an insignificant speck, on a tiny rock - spinning in an incomprehensibly vast universe. Why are we here?

My mind is currently out of control.

Time for work...

8.11PM

Called my dad - he seemed in good spirits. I'm pleased. He's a wonderful man and deserves to be happy. The house is calm. For now, my head isn't rushing. I walked through the door to be welcomed by a messy house. And two tired but beautiful ladies were greeted by an equally exhausted dad.

THURSDAY 5 JANUARY
5.40PM

Had a call from the doctor, something up with my bloods. It's either liver damage (which wouldn't be a surprise). Or diabetes, I assume... The irony is I currently feel good health-wise.

Also have a telephone assessment with our organisations' Occupational Health consultant tomorrow - another chance to dredge up the last two or twenty years of my life.

Oh, and the mortgage. My old provider gave the wrong settlement figure; again. It's keeping me awake at night. These two things are stoking my irrationality, self-loathing and paranoia. I need something to occupy my mind. I had an idea today for a second book - if I live to finish this one.

It's my daughter's birthday tomorrow. At least I bought her a nice present. My wife is totally prepared. She's truly amazing. I don't deserve her. If I die she can find someone better. Tomorrow will be so much fun. But my self-esteem is at rock-bottom.

8.30PM

My head's banging. I received a council tax letter. Not opened it. I imagine it's a missed payments demand. They'll be lucky. I'm skint.

My eyes are wide. My body is exhausted. The tank is empty. I'm feeling stressed; manic and wired.

FRIDAY 6 JANUARY – MY DAUGHTER'S BIRTHDAY
8.10PM

What. A. Day.

She was awash with presents and been hyperactive since 5.00am. And tired since midday - she's not the only one.

There are toys everywhere. She's such a lucky girl - utterly adored by everyone.

I've taken thousands of photos since she was born. There are only a handful of us together. As I'm the only one who-ever takes them.

My wife had to go to the doctor again. But she's fine. Mentally and physically she's strong - twenty days and counting.

The un-opened letter was junk from HMRC. Explaining how they are wasting my tax contributions. My obscene worrying and fretting are embarrassing. I've just read what I wrote yesterday. I was in a bad place. But I can't control it. I've tried. My mind runs free. But we should never discard our feelings, particularly bad ones. We need to make time to talk. Talking changes lives.

Occupational Health is closing my case. It was an expensive box ticking exercise; a waste of time and money.

All in all, it's been a lovely day. We've made some wonderful memories. We're ready for her party. I say we. I've done nothing. Sorry. I lied. I just signed for the cake that's just been delivered. That my wife selected and paid for. It's a shameful and embarrassing admission. What kind of dad and husband am I? If you suffer with self-loathing and low self-esteem, you'll know exactly how I feel right now.

My wife's struggling again but was up for it. My daughter? Well. She was fizzing all day. Like a firecracker. It was lovely seeing her playing with her friends. She's already laying the foundations for her life; at age three. It's staggering. I'm so proud. She's everything I hoped for, and so, so much more. Intelligent, wild, curious, rebellious, caring, loving and sensitive…

We spent all afternoon and evening playing - I can honestly say this is the best I've felt for a couple of months - which is surprising. As a couple of days ago I was low, and despondent. It's important to realise and enjoy when you're feeling good. Because it's impossible to know when the dark thoughts and mental self-harm will return.

Hard work rewarded

A spring in my step, the smile on my face,
Days now moving at a more relaxed pace
Are signs that I'm good, that my head is well,
Medication and therapy starting to gel

The result is I'm no longer just trying to cope,
It's such a nice feeling, to be filled with hope
That the good days won't end, that I will be fine,
And the sun in my life will continue to shine

SUNDAY 8 JANUARY
11.06PM

I've been up since three this morning. My daughter had a terrible night. My wife spent most of the day in bed. I cooked a roast dinner. Made sure she ate properly and kept up with the medication.

So, I looked after my daughter, and cleaned the house before the health visitor comes tomorrow. Not that it's dirty. I just want it to be spotless.

I hardly ate anything. I'll be seriously unwell if I carry this on. I need to sort my head out.

MONDAY 9 JANUARY
7.02AM

Have you ever been so tired you felt like you were going to puke? That's where I am. I barely said anything before work. Haven't eaten or drank anything yet either… I didn't even say goodbye to my daughter. Wow. What an arsehole.

5.45PM

The bus was late. My mortgage still isn't sorted. And my solicitors are not answering their phones… Had a text to say the council tax demand letter arrived. Now we're stuck in a massive traffic jam…

Fuck off world.

8.30PM

The health-care visit went okay. My wife's fine; just tired all the time. I'm so tired and short tempered. I have no patience. My body is heavy. I've got a booming headache. The house is a tip. Tonight? I don't care. Even writing is effort. Life is effort. It's horrible when we feel this way isn't it...

TUESDAY 10 JANUARY
6.40AM

I slept for eight hours. Feels like I blinked once. I'm exhausted and can see the strain if I look in the mirror. Starting to worry that people can see it when they look at me and I'll start getting the dreaded question 'Are you okay?' Thousands of times I've lied. I also wonder how many people genuinely care? What would some people do if I replied by saying *Well actually, I'm skint, tired and struggling with my mental health*. It's wrong, but I think sometimes a can of worms isn't worth opening. How many times have you done it? Maybe you're still doing it...

My asthma pump has run out. I can't even afford to replace it.

9.31PM

I phoned Nan. She's starting Chemo tomorrow. And will have people around her for the next few weeks. Dad's asked to meet me for a beer Saturday. I told Nan I loved her.

My daughter starts her new playgroup class tomorrow. She can't wait. She's ready.

I'm full of stress, anger and uncertainty. My parents gave me a lift home. Couldn't ask how they are. I'm at emotional capacity. I want to scream, shout, go for a run, get wasted, punch someone; turn a table over. I'm struggling.

WEDNESDAY 11 JANUARY

6.55AM

Twelve hours ago, I was at work. Now I'm at the train station on my way back. So many people look tired, stressed and unwell. It's very sad. You might be one of them? Currently I am.

My daughter's first day in her new class

My wife has two separate doctors' appointments

My nan goes in for chemo

Big day

8.28PM

My wife struggled moving around today, so I'm taking tomorrow off work. My heart is full of a love and admiration for her… Although if she crashes out I'll go fishing! I can't believe I wrote that. I almost deleted it.

Nan couldn't have all her treatment. She had a reaction to the chemo. It's no surprise.

I'm worried about my dad, who's looking after him? He's dealing with all this and holding everything and everyone together - as well as himself. What a man, my idol.

Me and my grandad, bless him, loved Only Fools and Horses. One of the best episodes is *Strained Relations*. That says it all. At my grandad's funeral the theme tune was played as his coffin was carried from the church to the funeral car. They nearly dropped the coffin on-route. It was both heart-breaking and hilarious.

My daughter had a good first day in her new class. But also fell down a few stairs. It was my fault. I couldn't get to her in time.

I'm lying on the floor typing. The baby monitor is next to me. For about the last hour and a half I've been watching her chest going up and down.

My fault
My guilt
My penance

THURSDAY 12 JANUARY
21.24

Luckily, she had a good night - slept well. At least that made one of us. Her chest is bruised. But she's fine.

I did housework all morning. My wife is finding basic tasks a struggle. I made sure the hospital bag was packed. As the morning wore on; I was getting worn out. And the guilt slowly ebbed away. Had a text from my mum saying *Don't feel guilty. Children are so quick, and accidents just happen. She will have a few more. But it hurts you as much as them xx.* Possibly the most profound thing she has ever said to me. She's so right. I was in pain long after my daughter had forgotten about it.

SNOW!

It came down heavy for a good couple of hours. My daughter was so excited, so we went for a snowball-filled walk!

Nan was in hospital again today. I haven't spoken to Dad. He doesn't need to be hassled. And repeatedly have the same painful conversation.

I finally sorted the council tax. No idea about the mortgage - nothing else to say. I'm hyper-sensitive. My self-esteem is low. I haven't looked in a mirror for days. I feel like there is nowhere to turn. Please try talking to someone if you're feeling like this.

FRIDAY 13 JANUARY
9.30PM

There was just enough snow when we got up for me and our eldest to build her first snowman in the garden. It's a day we'll never forget. My wife joined in at the end. And we got some lovely photos.

We should complete our mortgage on Tuesday. Great news on today of all days; the universe mocking me. Relief is coursing through my veins. The pressure in my head is easing. The vice is being loosened. It feels like the noose is too.

I'm so pleased I've been at home to take care of my wife these last few days. She is (and all expecting mums are) so amazing and courageous. The physical strain on her body must be immense. I'm doing my best to look after both my beautiful ladies.

Watching a programme called '*A Good Day to Die: Fake Funerals in South Korea*'. A business is now offering people 'fake funerals' to help them deal with the pressure of life. Participants put on burial clothes, enter a casket, and experience death. It seems nuts to me. But you do what you need to do. Nobody should question the coping mechanisms of others when they don't impact on anyone else.

In South Korea, apparently the need to succeed in business has contributed to catastrophic levels of depression. As I write this, forty-two South Korean people are taking their lives every day. It's unspeakably tragic... People in power need to help them, now.

Nobody should be made to feel like their only hope, and only option, is eternal oblivion. It breaks my heart to think so many people are so unhappy.

Your place of work should not make you feel depressed. It's the same with home-life. I'm not saying you can wave a wand, and everything will go away. It won't. And that would be disrespectful anyhow. Very few people know what I, and you, are really going through. We just don't let many in people in, eh? But I have some control and so do you. That's why I walked away from my first marriage. Of course, I felt like a failure. Like everyone was laughing at me. But now I'm one of the lucky ones - despite my demons.

Depression

Depression is a common mental disorder that causes people to experience depressed mood, loss of interest or pleasure, feelings of guilt or low self-worth, disturbed sleep or appetite, low energy, and poor concentration. Depression is different from feeling down or sad. Unhappiness is something which everyone feels at one time or another, usually due to a particular cause. A person experiencing depression will experience intense emotions of anxiety, hopelessness, negativity and helplessness, and the feelings stay with them instead of going away (Source: Mental Health Foundation website)

SATURDAY 14 JANUARY
9.06PM

My wife had an awful day. I feel helpless. No matter how much I do it doesn't feel enough. But this is not about me.

Tomorrow is the baby shower. I've already found out one of her best friends is not coming. The guilt and self-loathing are back. Now I think I should have done more. If it's not what she wants - it's my fault. Nothing I can do now. Apart from prepare my apologies. Don't get me wrong. I'm sincerely grateful her friends are organising this for her. This is just another example of the impossible standards I set myself - now I think I'm a bad person for caring... Enough of this mind-bending paranoia and mania...

I had a nice time with my dad. Nan seems okay. Cancer is evil. So many of you reading this know exactly how I feel.

SUNDAY 15 JANUARY
8.00PM

My wife loved her baby shower. She came back with so many gifts. She's so lucky. I'm so grateful to her friend (you know who you are x) for organising it.

The last four days have been life-sapping. But you just keep going, don't you? You don't give up just because things are hard, do you? My wife is frustrated because she can't do much. I've got to keep on top of things. I don't want her stress levels and blood pressure to rise. Nothing I can do about mine.

Eleven days to go...

MONDAY 16 JANUARY
7.20AM

My daughter was awake between one and four o'clock this morning. Broken nights are brutal, aren't they?

Here we go: Mortgage completion; getting a loan. Borrowing some money off my dad and paying Nan back - and clearing my council tax debt. Paying for my wife's ring and buying last minute baby stuff. It sounds overwhelming doesn't it? But today, for once, my thought processes are clear. I know what I'm doing.

I've still not updated my CV.

Mortgage should complete tomorrow. After all the stress, anger, frustration, and yeah; some tears. Christmas was horrible financially. I was very low. Felt worthless - hated myself. Today I just feel relief.

I might even sleep properly tonight.

TUESDAY 17 JANUARY
6.15PM

What a terrible night – my wife could barely move this morning, so I didn't go to work; again. I need to get back to work. That means help from grandparents.

The mortgage completed. Funds should be in the bank by the end of the week. Made my loan application today - same applies.

No bad dreams recently - self-loathing yes; suicidal thoughts; no. Or should I say, thoughts about how much better people would be without me.

But…

For the last week or so every time I've taken a large knife from the dishwasher I've thought about jamming it in my stomach. Not normal is it? No idea why it started. I'm not going to act on it. As far as I know. It's dark - and strange. But I'm not going back to my therapist. No way.

My daughter gets more beautiful but naughty every day. But I like that she pushes boundaries. It shows emotional intelligence, and intellectual curiosity.

WEDNESDAY 18 JANUARY

7.05AM

My wife is basically housebound. She struggles walking short distances. Our parents are now helping with nursery runs. We'd be stuffed without them... It's hard - but not pregnancy hard.

I feel like I'm losing weight. But still feel and look enormous. I hate myself and my body. I'm repulsive.

9.00PM

Had a chat about the book with an old friend and work colleague. We talked about focus. The combination of fatherhood and mental health is crucial.

I don't want to dilute the mental health focus. I want to confront it. Embrace the issues. Challenge the stigma. And show how people live and manage mental health. I don't want to lose the intimacy. Or the connection I want to build with you. It's not my life. It's far bigger and more important... It's our lives.

It's the first time I've thought properly about being a dad again. If you are one, you know how privileged you feel. It's the most important thing I'll ever do. It's also a reality check. I count myself blessed. I have a lovely house; an amazing wife and a beautiful daughter. I can't wait - my only hope? Neither of my daughters ever suffers with mental illness. I'd triple how bad my problems are if it meant my daughters never have to feel that pain for one day. I'm not special. It's just a parent thing.

It's getting so close. I can already smell the piles of dirty nappies. And hear the hungry crying.

It's Only Fools and Horses again! *Second Time Around* – Thank you John Sullivan.

9.00PM

The mortgage company sent me a cheque! But things are coming together. Everyone is asking me about the baby. I forgot what that's like. I'm getting excited. I want to welcome our new daughter into the world. The day our first was born I cried so much. For hours, I could hear my heart pounding. The adrenaline produced a natural high chemists' will never replicate.

We're ready for the hospital. The bag is packed. Everything is covered. The nursery looks lovely.

Loan sorted; paid my council tax. I'm getting myself sorted. Called my nan - she sounded better. I said we'll visit soon. I want her to meet our new arrival as soon as possible. It's so sad my grandad won't. We'll take her to the cemetery.

I'll treat myself to a nice beer tomorrow night. I think I deserve it.

Mad, sad, dysfunctional dad

Not running away, but feeling so mad,
Dealing with feelings I've always had

But tried to deny, by shrugging my shoulders
But denial made it worse as I got older

Until the dark clouds blurred my vision
Then I realised the size of my mission

To let people in, and talk about feelings
And repair relationships, start the healing,

With the help of friends, family and darling wife
I'm striving to bring smiles back into my life

And of others too, as it's totally unfair
To expect them to live with my pain and bare,

The brunt of my illness and all of my crap
While I'm figuring out my true life map

I guess what I'm saying is I love who I am
In spite of the illness that make me that man....

A mad, sad, dysfunctional dad

SATURDAY 21 JANUARY
9.19PM

Collected the eternity ring... She's been the most spectacular girlfriend, fiancée, wife and mummy. I'd have given her more gifts like this if I could've afforded it. She deserves more than I'll ever be able to give her.

Finances pretty much sorted. Now focusing on fatherhood... Her tummy is so big. When our baby kicks it looks like a Mexican wave.

I've spent the last day and a half cleaning. The house smells clean. It's nice. I'm a Liverpool nut. Ask anyone. Travelled to the Ataturk in 2005 for The Champions League Final... Solo. We were breathtaking that night. Today, we were shambolic. But I'm in love with football again.

My daughter now knows what's happening. And wondering why we're still waiting!

SUNDAY 22 JANUARY
7.02PM

Drank too much wine last night and woke up steaming.

Had some extremely insightful feedback about the first part of the book today... From my Portugal based, northern brethren. He's the first person to read any of this. And one of only two people who I've sent it to.

After soft play my daughter asked to go to a restaurant for

pizza. We had so much fun. It was a shame Mummy wasn't with us. She can't really drive. Or walk any distance. Wondering if I think it is my fault and that I'm a failure? You'd be right. I'm livid with myself. Couldn't even look after my wife during her pregnancy, could I?

MONDAY 23 JANUARY
8.26PM

I'm shattered, very long day. Loads to do at work, no time. I need to stay at home tomorrow to look after my daughter. Her eczema is flaring up. I feel so sorry for her. But she copes with it amazingly.

I've barely managed to eat. Three days until our due date. Memories of the maternity room are flooding back.

TUESDAY 24 JANUARY
6.10PM

My daughter needs hydrocortisone cream. After the doctor we all went to meet one of my sisters for brunch in Canterbury. We had a good chat, including about my therapy sessions - I told her to call me if she ever needs me.

The sessions were about sixty minutes each. They only work if you engage. There's no quick fix.

Initially I had to go back to my earliest memories. Good and bad. And then slowly identify all the trigger points which have affected me.

The first couple of sessions were focused on relationships with my parents, and how their relationships with my sisters affected me. I had a very fractious relationship with everyone in my house for some time, for various reasons. We identified my trust issues, particularly with women. I've been treated badly by women - which damaged me a tad. But treated them shockingly too.

In trying to compromise I developed co-dependency disorder, which made me worse. Then there was the resentment I felt towards my parents when I was made to come home from France at the end of my college course. It turns out I carried that for years. I spent most of the first two sessions in tears. And I never went straight home. I needed time to collect my thoughts. We also talked about meds. When I first went to the doctor I was prescribed mood immobilisers - basically drugs that stop you feeling anything. I wasn't prepared to lose that part of me. That's why I chose herbal remedies and therapy.

The next sessions were about my own stuff. The impossible standards I compare myself against. And set. The distorted view I have of myself. And my self-esteem issues – which was non-existent when I started therapy and had been for some time.

We discussed my teenage years and early twenties. How my relationships had been pretty rubbish – and how when I did finally find someone I treated her disgracefully. Especially as I knew she loved me. I had loads of acquaintances, but few real friends. I didn't let anyone in - hiding at the bottom of a bottle.

It was hard to admit I hated myself. And felt utterly worthless; undeserving of life.

The sessions were hard and contained a lot of silence - it's those periods of introspection, when you must look deep inside yourself that are the worst - horrible.

Just as hard is then explaining things to your nearest and dearest; being totally vulnerable. You become wracked with crippling paranoia and ludicrous irrationality. What will people say when we're not around? Will people treat us differently? Will people even believe us? We all go through it.

The last two sessions were person centred. What do I need to do? What changes must I try and make?

Being selfish normally has negative connotations. But that's exactly what I had to do. Why not try it, even if it just means taking some time each day to look after yourself (which I rarely do). I'd spent years trying to solve other people's problems - when I was an absolute mess; and getting worse.

The only person who really looks after you is you. Even your wife, best mate, parents or professional network can only do so much. I also had to stop feeling so guilty for every little thing. I expect far more from me than others do. This is still one of my biggest struggles.

Now I'm trying to put myself first a bit more. And I'm slowly becoming a better father, husband, son, brother and friend. I'm nowhere near the finished article – we all have good days - and some of us very bad days. Certainly, the thoughts of ending things are not currently in the equation. I'm trying hard to rebuild relationships I've damaged, but on my own terms.

When I started therapy I did a relationship spider. You put yourself at centre. Then write the names of the people in relation to how close you are to them. It showed that my focus was on things farthest away from me. At the end of my last session we did this again. I'd switched my focus to me and the things closest to me. It sounds straightforward doesn't it? That's the frustrating thing. It really wasn't. But that was, and still is, part of my illness.

(No) building blocks

Trust is earned over periods of time,
And knowing it's there, is truly sublime

Knowing someone is there, sharing your pain,
Gives people security that's hard to explain,

But what if life shatters this from the start?
And ruins relationships in full and in part?

There is one positive, despite feeling so blue,
Not the only one screwing things up is you

DUE DATE TOMORROW

I'm full of nervous energy. But it's not the same as the first time. Then I had no idea how we'd manage. It was exciting and terrifying. Now I know what to expect. We've also got amazing family around us too. Not everyone is as lucky.

I hope the birth is easier for my wife though. She was in labour thirty hours first time round - then got a serious infection but was discharged anyway. Two days later we went back to hospital. And were told we should never have left in the first place. It was midnight. We were prescribed medication the hospital didn't have - then told to drive to a twenty-four-hour, pharmacy ten minutes away. When we got there? It was shut. I was raging. I wanted to go back to the hospital but was advised not to. Probably wise. I'd have ended up getting arrested.

But the nurses were wonderful - kind, thoughtful, helpful, empathetic and caring.

My wife was very poorly for about two weeks. I did everything I could. Maybe that's why my bond with my daughter is so strong... It broke my heart. But I looked after them with the help of our parents.

I've already promised myself and my wife I won't let the same things happen again.

THURSDAY 26 JANUARY
11.00PM - DUE DATE

Very few babies are born on their due date. Neither was ours.

This time we've discussed so many things - getting routines in earlier. Doing controlled crying earlier if we need to. (One of the most horrible experiences ever - me? I sobbed the first few times. I hated it. And often wanted to hurt myself to make myself feel better) - all you want to do is burst in and smother them with love.

We'll hopefully be welcoming our new arrival into a world of calm. *Not chaos.*

FRIDAY 27 JANUARY - 21.25PM
ONE DAY OVERDUE

I've been feeling sick most of the day and had the runs. The last time I felt like this was on my fateful thirtieth birthday trip to Leeds. Why was it a fateful trip? I'll tell you – I wasn't supposed to be there...

After separating from my ex-wife, this birthday was supposed to be a watershed. So, I booked a trip to Bin El Ouidane; a beautiful lake in the heart of the Atlas Mountains - 15,000 acres and full of carp. My flight was on 04.03.2009 at 00.00hrs. I arrived on the wrong day, it was the night before. Stranded at Stansted Airport I did the only rational thing: Got trashed then travelled to Leeds with over a grand in my sky rocket - to see my dear friends who I met whilst I'd been travelling in South America. They are genuinely lovely people. I partied until my body was a write off. Then I travelled home.

So, one evening while there I took my mate's beautiful housemate to dinner. Walking home my guts started turning over. As soon as everyone went to bed I went to the toilet. And literally did not move for about two hours. I decided to crash on the sofa - on a thick towel. I fell asleep. But woke up shortly afterwards to find I'd messed myself. Maybe the worst food poisoning I've ever had. I put a load of washing on immediately and scrubbed the sofa down. I'm not sure if I've ever told him this… Sorry mate.

It surely can't be long now. I've been awake since half past two this morning.

SATURDAY 28 JANUARY - 8.12PM
TWO DAYS OVERDUE

I honestly thought we'd have our new baby by now. Not even had any little signs. Trying to work, clean and look after everyone is impossible. It's taking its toll on both of us. I feel at emotional capacity

SUNDAY 29 JANUARY - 8.35PM
THREE DAYS OVERDUE

Can't face work tomorrow - I want to be at home with my wife. If I was wealthy I wouldn't be working. I don't mean ever. Just until the birth. But I've no choice. Most of us are only one missed rent or mortgage payment from losing our homes, aren't we? Nothing like living in continuous financial insecurity to ease the mind...

I finally paid Nan back - the relief is indescribable. Now I can focus completely on my family. The pieces are slowly coming together. I feel like the head of the house - the provider. Like it should be when your wife is about to give birth.

Soon our family will be complete.

MONDAY 30 JANUARY - 8.36PM
FOUR DAYS OVERDUE

Still no sign, I'm lying on the sofa knackered. My wife...? She must be fifty times worse. Every day is more of a struggle. I've got tomorrow off. But I'll be amazed if anything happens.

TUESDAY 31 JANUARY – 7.45PM
FIVE DAYS OVERDUE

Both our daughters won't be born in January. But I honestly don't know how much more my wife can take. I've no idea how she's coping. I'm bad enough. This pregnancy has been immeasurably harder than first time around. At least if this is a sign of things to come we're ready. The first time my sole focus was my wife. Last minute runs to the supermarket on a Sunday afternoon for chocolate. Running her baths and cooking huge Sunday roasts. And duvet days - it was serene in a way.

We're blessed to be having our second child. But the last week has been one of the hardest I've experienced. Hopefully this will soon be replaced by crying, feeds, and messy nappies. But best of all, new baby hugs and smiles.

THREE. BLESSED AGAIN

WEDNESDAY 1 FEBRUARY – 7.43PM
SIX DAYS OVERDUE

Midwife today. We got to listen to a strong heartbeat – a crazy miracle isn't it? It bends my head trying to think what it's like for a baby - half way between life and the oblivion of non-existence.

I baked with my daughter for the first time today. It was very basic, but so much fun. I'm hoping in a few years she'll be doing this with her little sister. We're still undecided on a name.

The dreams have started again. Not being murdered - but one very vivid dream. In which my mother-in-law berates me for being a failure, both as a father and husband. *She's never done this*. I've spent days and insomnia-fuelled nights thinking I could have done more. It's started again. I need to be careful...

THURSDAY 2 FEBRUARY - 7.45AM
SIX DAYS OVERDUE

We're in the delivery room - been at hospital for three hours. Thought we were in business. But looks like a false alarm... But baby's vital signs are perfect, so I shouldn't whinge - stupid twat.

Looks like we'll be off home soon – luckily our daughter is in nursery.

3.00PM

Back at home. My wife's in bed. I'm lying on the floor watching a documentary. It's surreal. The amount of time I've spent in this exact position. Either writing this; watching documentaries or sport - sometimes drinking. There's a groove in the carpet. There are certainly some stains where I've spilled food and booted drinks over.

6.15PM

We've been timing contractions for three and a half hours.

FRIDAY 3 FEBRUARY
1.15AM

Our wait is over! Our new arrival was born at 10.25pm last night; weighing an awesome ten pounds six ounces. She's amazing, simply stunning. Of course, it's dad's bias. But she totally is. And nearly the length of the delivery room crib!

It was a very dangerous delivery. My wife lost more than three pints of blood. I have never seen anything as bad in my life. She didn't even have time for an epidural. But that was the fault of the midwife. She was in agony. And they did nothing. I'm still seething.

She could have died. If we'd got stuck in traffic, there's no way we could have done anything. It makes me shudder. But the aftercare at the hospital was incredible. The team were amazing. They saved the life of my wife and new-born baby. I'm forever grateful to them x

It's incredible holding a baby in your arms for the first time…

The most amazing experiences of my life; the birth of my daughters…

My greatest gifts

A cry, a whimper, eyes shut, fists clenched
Wrapped in a blanket, so tiny, my beautiful baby,
I stare at her, heart; full of love, cheeks drenched
Those first seconds, the first cuddle, indescribable, crazy.

I didn't blink, or move, heart melting like butter
A twitch, a scream, and a cry for a feed
Then the magical moment, her eyes start to flutter
As they open, her first vision, so blurry, is me

Our first cuddle, so precious, our beautiful baby so fragile
The nurse, so elated, asks about names,
I glanced at my wife, lovingly, knowingly with a smile
From this moment, our lives, never the same

(A connection, a bond, I've never felt in my life
Well just once, the first time I saw my wife.)

FRIDAY 3 FEBRUARY

6.05PM

Mummy and baby are home safely after twelve hours of observations.

Bubba (our pet name) is eating and pooping well. Still not twenty-four hours old. She's very chilled out. I've been awake for forty hours. Twice at the hospital I walked into the wrong maternity suite. Surprised they didn't think I was some sort of pervert and call the police.

The bedroom is quiet for now. It's time to rest. I'm the luckiest man in the world.

SATURDAY 4 FEBRUARY

2.15AM

It's been a rough day and night. For about eight hours Bubba would not eat and had bone-dry nappies. She was very stressed out. Not the only one...

We called the hospital and my wife spoke to the on-call midwife. And we booked a visit for later today. After Bubba had been properly winded and had some formula. Then all three of my beautiful ladies finally crashed out.

I had a cup of tea with my mother-in-law before she left. I'm so grateful to her for being there for us. She's an amazing lady.

SUNDAY 5 FEBRUARY

7.15PM

The house is silent; but for how long…?

Midwife said my wife will take about six weeks to heal. She'll need loads of support. Bubba's check-up went well. She's just perfect. She can already grab my finger. Her hugs could defrost a freezer. But her nappies could wilt a flower.

It's my responsibility to make sure we get through this. I can do my recovery on my own time.

So, how's our eldest? Nobody can know how hard it is for her. What she is going through. How she really feels. She's only three! I wish I knew. It breaks my heart, the thought that she doesn't feel loved. I hate the guilt and feeling a failure… She's going through a life-changing event. She is no longer the sole focus of our attention. Mummy can't do anything with her. And I'm trying to make sure everything gets done. And everyone feels equally loved.

MONDAY 6 FEBRUARY

8.55PM

I woke up about 5.45am this morning after very little sleep. I passed out on the sofa at about half four - with our eldest on the sofa wrapped in blankets. We are all exhausted. I need to keep going.

The midwife said my wife may have torn pelvic ligaments. If that's the case, it'll take months to heal. I've asked her to speak to the midwife tomorrow. The truth is I'm terrified. I'm lying on the sofa in the dark in the living room. Bubba's in her crib. I also have our eldest's monitor. My wife has been sleeping since seven o'clock. She's exhausted and emotional, so having a night off. Me? For now, it doesn't matter how I feel or what I want. As the partner it's just what we do, right?

I'm hoping the midwife will ask my wife to go back to the hospital. Seeing someone you love in so much pain. It breaks your heart, right? It's breaking mine. But I can't show it.

Bubba's developing well. Looking round and trying to roll – and giving little cuddles. Our eldest is warming to Bubba and was so sweet today. When Bubba cried she tried to make it better. In such a stretched environment, sharing these moments is so important. It relieves the pressure.

So, the big question, fatherhood and mental health? So far, I'm holding my own; just...

TUESDAY 7 FEBRUARY
2.35PM

My wife has another medical issue so more antibiotics. She doesn't need this. Midwife coming again Thursday. Bubba's checks were fine. She's perfect.

My wife still needs lots of care and love. All new mums do, don't they? But, we're on the slow road to recovery. She's having her post-natal depression questionnaire/visit next week. When she did it after our eldest was born I went out. I'll do so again.

She needs space, so she can be honest. I don't care what she says, as long as it helps her. Nothing else matters.

4.29PM

Just realised... Not showered since Wednesday. It's Tuesday - unselfish? Or plain disgusting?

8.15PM

Bubba has a cold - sounds so bunged up. Just had a bottle so hoping she'll kip for an hour or so. None for me though. Want to keep an eye on her breathing. Mummy went up an hour ago...

Our eldest...?

She is starting to develop her relationship with our little Bubba. It's lovely to see. Not having visitors is really helping. We're bonding. My wife is still poorly but getting involved as much as she can.

I'm buzzing - but exhausted. I'm getting into a groove. And everyone is benefiting. When I first started writing this? I was worried, fragile, and scared I'd struggle to cope. Currently I'm flying... But some planes crash.

WEDNESDAY 8 FEBRUARY
7.25AM

I'm in trouble. It's my swearing. The last couple of weeks it's got worse. Recently our eldest said 'crap'. Her first swear word.

I kept it to myself.... But she said another one today. I've often been asked to leave a boozer due to my potty mouth - proud? Nah... Honest? Why should I be anything else? Lies catch up with us all in the end. And the longer it takes; the more pain it creates.

Recently I was talking to a close friend. He asked me if raising a family is financially challenging. What would you say? I said yes, of course it is. But you know that when you decide to have a family don't you?

Some people have children. Some people have wealth. Very few have both. Given the choice? I'd choose children - every time.

10.15PM

So, it's night three of me and Bubba downstairs. I have our eldest's monitor in the corner. The result has been two good nights for Mummy. And she's looking better for it. But her movement is still limited.

Our eldest has been very demanding; fighting for my attention. I'm trying to show her she doesn't need to. I've felt the guilt (and other stuff), like all parents.

THURSDAY 9 FEBRUARY
8.46PM

Midwife wasn't happy. My wife had to go back to the doctor. We're all up in the bedroom. Bubba's not settling - maybe it's the new surroundings. My wife is exhausted. She can barely get out of bed. I'm spent, empty; bereft. I need sleep and am barely eating. I'm also drinking more coffee. It's affecting me. And I don't like it. Fatherhood is wonderful. But can grind you down. Maybe it's done so to you. It is, me.

My nan's chemo has stopped.

10.15PM

It's going to be a long night. Bubba's refusing to sleep. It's just relentless crying. So, time for yet another bottle. With how much she's already eaten I can't believe she's hungry. But I'm wrong. – Unbelievable.

Somehow our eldest is managing to sleep through this. Who knows about the neighbours? Who cares? Suppose we'll find out tomorrow....

FRIDAY 10 FEBRUARY
7.40PM

Bubba had a bad start to the night - but then slept from half eleven until five this morning. I still woke up with a head like the worst possible hangover.

The family is bonding nicely. We compared newborn photos earlier. It's incredible how much they look alike at birth. Our eldest went to Nanny and Grandad's for the weekend - I'm so grateful to our parents. They're making a huge difference to our lives.

Tomorrow I'm out with the boys. My wife's getting better so I'm not feeling too guilty, but that'll change. I can't hold it off for long. And alcohol doesn't help either does it?

SATURDAY 11 FEBRUARY
5.00PM

Two legs of today's merriment down. Met the boys at lunch and was on top form. Felt a little like my old self. Plenty of beer - loads of laughs.

Then I met one of my sisters at a wicked little bar in the city. The drinks were fabulous. The food was delicious. We had a lovely couple of hours together...

Here we go... My mate has just turned up. It's time for Wales vs England (rugby); Liverpool vs Tottenham, then Ross Noble. I'm feeling rather drunk already. It's been a nice day so far...

SUNDAY 12 FEBRUARY
7.00PM

What a shocking hangover I had this morning... We didn't make it to the end of the gig. What we watched was hilarious though. I'm so grateful to my wife for organising everything.

At the boozer showing the sport... It got messy; coffee Tequila in abundance. England and Liverpool both won. Shot some pool. The boozer was heaving. It was like a window into my past. I was buzzing by the time we left.

This afternoon I cooked a textbook roast; and my parents came. Our eldest came back with a bruise on her face. Fell off the sofa at their house. Not impressed. Dad's transferring the money next weekend. I'm so grateful. It'll give us a safety net during the last three months of my wife's maternity.

Bubba has just gone down. The hangover has finally gone. It's time for bed.

MONDAY 13 FEBRUARY
8.27PM

Bubba's cough has been getting worse all day.

My wife has a doctors' appointment tomorrow. She doesn't deserve to feel like this. I can only do so much. Even that isn't enough.

It's the most tired I've felt since Bubba was born. We're all feeling it. Our eldest had a terrible night. I was in her bedroom until half eleven bless her. She was really under the weather and just wanted cuddles. I can't blame her. She's still adjusting to such a huge change in her life.

Bubba's calling…

Not Pirate Material, Brighton Material.

In my youth I travelled down to Brighton;
Looking for inspiration and enlightenment

Selfish actions of women I trusted
Left a strong man emotionally busted

Head mangled, a broken soul;
who'd lost all hope and trust

Bad experiences taken their toll
It felt like a time of shit or bust

It wasn't an epic epiphany
But did create new feelings in me

That made the rough not seem so tough
Days later I felt my best *was* good enough

That's it's always possible to dream and achieve
As long as you stay strong, stay true and believe

In the kindness and goodness of you fellow man
For the entirety of your earth life span

Never felt like it was a group for the elite
But for the man on the street

Thank you, Mike, and everyone

ST. VALENTINE'S DAY
8.38PM

Mummy was exhausted last night so I took Bubba downstairs. Her cough was bad. I spent ages just cuddling her. Then made her bed elevated to combat the phlegm. It was worth it. She slept surprisingly well. I got about four hours.

Our eldest slept during the day. Can't remember the last time she did. Bubba slept loads. Both had coughs and temperatures. It was hard seeing them like that. I wanted to cry. The midwife was happy. Bubba's inching closer to birth weight.

Still concerned about my wife; she's continuing to be monitored. She doesn't look right. It must be so hard. She's got no time to convalesce.

But she still got me a lovely card. I gave her a present early. A miracle!

Writing is hard. Mentally and emotionally I'm struggling. I can feel myself slipping...

WEDNESDAY 15 FEBRUARY
8.35PM

I looked after my ladies who woke up throughout another awful night.

Initially Bubba didn't settle anyway. Up and down all night. The last time was 2.45am. She woke up at 7.00am. Our eldest didn't go to nursery - clearly not right; and off her food.

It was a milestone day. At just before midday we registered our little Bubba's birth. She's utterly beautiful – Just like her sister and mummy. I'm an incredibly lucky man.

Our eldest asked to go to bed early again. Did she settle? I think you know the answer. She's now asleep on the sofa next to me. At least my other two are down. I'm exhausted - and currently using that word a lot.

I think the television is annoying my eldest. But I can't lay in the dark wide awake. I hate it. My mind races and takes me over. My thoughts become uncontrollable. Is my nan dying? What happens when we die? I contemplate eternal oblivion. What on earth is that like? I think about how soon after people die they are forgotten. Only the exceptionally good, or exceptionally bad are remembered. Serial killers and mass murderers are glamorised and studied. I've watched many, many documentaries on such people. They're wired differently to pretty much everybody else. No empathy. No value of life. No compassion. My God - where did that digression come from?

What will happen if I lose my job? How would we pay the mortgage? If I died would my wife be better off without me? Would she be better off without me now? What happens if the girls are bullied at school or don't make friends? It makes me shudder. It bends my fucking head. But money means nothing when you're dead.

I'm sure you've been through many of these emotions, so just remember you're not alone. And if it troubles you too much, get help. Don't suffer in silence.

The house is silent. I've muted the television while I'm writing. Hopefully the illness will start to recede. I wish my hair wouldn't.

THURSDAY 16 FEBRUARY
11.50AM

Proper bad night - had to bring our eldest down again. She slept on the sofa; me on the floor. I think she slept okay from midnight onwards. I didn't.

Midwife came. Bubba's back to her birth weight. They've both been discharged. Mummy is doing amazing. She's a staggering lady.

Our eldest now has tonsillitis. Her temperature was over thirty-nine degrees. She was so upset. It's no surprise is it? She's only three. Little Bubba at least seems to be slowly kicking her cough. Doctor said her chest is clear. We just need to keep an eye on her.

My mother-in-law came today. Said my wife is looking better. And I looked awful. Correct.

FRIDAY 17 FEBRUARY
7.03PM

It was another bad night. How many is that...? Our eldest has only just started her antibiotics. It'll take twenty-four hours to take effect. Nothing has changed for me. Tiredness is my onesie.

She's been stuttering for about a week. But today it was much worse. I'm in bits. I wonder if it's because of my parenting.... Have I been too strict? Have I neglected her since Bubba was born? Has my mental health affected her? Who knows? I know one thing though. I blame myself and feel sick. I just want to hurt myself. I'm restless. I'm manic.

I had a terrible stutter as a child. The bullying crushed me. I had to have speech therapy…. I'm so worried. I don't want her to go through what I did - feeling like a failure, being different, struggling with relationships, feeling inadequate.

It's breaking my heart writing this. I feel powerless, but totally responsible. We're having a consultation Monday. It's important I do everything I can to make sure she feels loved and supported. I want to protect her. And make everything better. I'm doing everything I can.

Reality check

What hurts more, punch or hateful word?
Most people's answer, well that's just absurd!

I tell you what, at nineteen stone
Knuckles don't hurt, like someone's tone.

SATURDAY 18 FEBRUARY
8.40PM

The nights aren't getting better. This morning was a train-wreck. Our eldest wanted to go out so we went into town. The minute we got there; both girls went ballistic. While walking through town we got some looks from other people as though to say *What horrible parents you are. What are you doing?* Why do people think they have the right to look at other people like that? And judge? Frankly - it's fuck all to do with them. And maybe people should concentrate on their own lives. Or maybe they don't have lives. Maybe that's the point?

My wife did some gardening yesterday… Today she's suffering. I'm a lot angrier than I let on. I've put my foot down. No physical exertion for a few days. I will not let her end up back in hospital; over my dead body.

Time seems to be passing at an accelerated rate. It's scary. A day passes in the blink of an eye. Bubba is already fifteen days old. It's been a blur of joy, tears, photographs and cuddles, beaming smiles, midwife visits, caffeine and medication. Broken sleep and broken dreams.

And diary entries.

SUNDAY 19 FEBRUARY
8.17PM – MY SISTER'S SURPRISE

Can't remember when I last woke up without a headache.

Anyway - a text out of the blue – my sister's boyfriend proposed to her. They've been together for seven years. She's over the moon. It makes me so happy.

I proposed to my wife on our first trip to Jamaica. There was a romantic little gazebo on the beach. So, while we were having afternoon drinks I was liaising with the hotel manager to help me. My cover story you ask? I said I was dashing off because I had bad food poisoning…. How romantic!

At one point I came back to see her being chatted up by an Italian guy. Wearing speedos; sandals and dark shades. Hilarious! Anyway, I managed to get everything sorted. And at sunset suggested we go a romantic walk. As we got to the bottom of the steps, she looked up and saw the path illuminated by candles both sides all the way to the gazebo and up the steps - to our candle-lit table. We had a meal, champagne and private waiter service. It was lush. She looked utterly stunning. (And still is today). When she said yes, my life at that point was complete. She'd made me the happiest man in the world, for the first time. Second time was when we got married. Third time was when our eldest was born. Fourth time was when Bubba was born. I just hope she feels she is getting as much from our relationship as I am. She deserves everything. She deserves the best.

Our eldest is struggling at bed time. She tells me she is going to cry as soon as I close the door. And she does. Basically, she thinks because Mummy, Daddy and Bubba share a room, and she's on her own, we don't love her.

She must be feeling vulnerable and unsettled. We must make sure she feels totally included in things. I don't want this to worsen her stutter. Or make her resent our little Bubba.

My body and mind are burning out. I've ripped my side lifting our eldest (it's because I'm out of shape) and busted my foot. My mind is being pummelled with parenting. I'm being so strict with her. She's started to tell me she doesn't like me. It makes me feel worthless. Wouldn't it you?

My biggest current challenge is helping her understand the difference between being told off and being told she can't have something. At present, she thinks I'm telling her off every time I speak to her. Hardly surprising she's not fond of me. But being a good dad is hard isn't it? You need unwavering self-belief. Otherwise you won't pull it off. You also need support. My wife is backing me up. So are our parents. But in quiet moments I doubt myself. I worry if I'm seriously damaging my relationship with my eldest - which horrifies me.

Spoke to the doctor about her stutter. We need to monitor it for the next two weeks. And book an appointment if it's no better. I'm being so careful. I can't let this escalate. Luckily, she's still okay in herself. I'm just praying it doesn't start getting her down. She has such a beautiful, caring, funny, sharp person-ality. I don't want it to be damaged. I'd be heartbroken. I'd take any illness if it meant my wife and daughters could live healthy, stress-free lives. I've lived around cancer, dementia, autism, severe mental illness, self-harm, addictions and eating disorders. And I mean it. I'd take anything for my three ladies - in a heartbeat.

We had a nice trip to the garden centre. Walking through the trees reminded me of when I worked at a farm with my mum and nan in a beautiful little village not far from us. I was good friends with one of the farmer's daughters; who was hot. I used to do fruit picking. And was paid in cash – a brown envelope every Friday; I felt like a king.

TUESDAY 21 FEBRUARY
9.40PM

Our eldest is becoming increasingly jealous and throwing tantrums. Especially when I explain that Bubba needs feeding and changing lots of the time - time which is being taken from her. She can see it and doesn't like it. I tell her I love her every day, and how proud we are of her.

Her stutter seems better today. I'll speak to the nursery tomorrow. And get an update on Friday. If they say it's still bad I'm calling the doctor. My wife is now the person I'm least worried about.

My head's a mess. There's been so much sickness in the house. We've not got routines in place as I'd like. It's making me anxious. Once I go back to work I'll have no control, or influence. I'll also not be bonding with my girls as much. It's sad to think about……. Work to live. Not live to work.

WEDNESDAY 22 FEBRUARY
8.38PM

Our eldest finally went back to nursery after an awful night. So much coughing and crying - it was horrible for both of us. But she ate well today and went to soft play after nursery. Both signs she's getting her mojo back. As I'm writing she's started coughing. I hope she settles down. I can't handle many more broken and restless nights.

We finally visited my wife's grandad. He's such a lovely bloke - eighty-nine years young this year. He was in good spirits and looked as good as I've seen him in a while. I got some lovely photos too. I'm building a catalogue like I did with our eldest. Each moment is precious. I don't want to miss one. You can't get them back.

THURSDAY 23 FEBRUARY
8.30PM

I finally had a bit of a rest as our eldest was at nursery - loads of housework of course. But it was easier with just Bubba to look after.

Our eldest's stutter hasn't improved. It makes me love her even more. You just want to protect your children, right? I've made a doctor's appointment for two weeks' time.

We're *still* trying to get Bubba's hip alignment appointment sorted. Hospital should've done it automatically due to her birth weight. Hospital said they'd call back. Did they? No. So I'll have to call them tomorrow.

My wife said I look exhausted. She's going to her mums tomorrow for some sort of post-baby shower. I said I'm not going. I'm not feeling sociable. It's one of my main symptoms. I withdraw.

FRIDAY 24 FEBRUARY

00.55AM

My wife did her baby thing; I'm pleased I didn't go - horrible eh? It's just people wanting to celebrate Bubba's birth. Shouldn't be feeling like that.

Not heard back from the hospital. I'll call them tomorrow. I shouldn't have to.

It's my sister's birthday tomorrow so we popped round today to see her. Our children had a play-date. My wife was struggling so I did the girls for the first half of the night. Just taken Bubba up but now I'm wide awake. It's bollocks.

I was thinking about playing online poker again. Even went onto the website and did some browsing. I used to play loads when I was married to my ex-wife and won quite a bit of money. But I knocked all that on the head when I left her. I've barely gambled since - I've too much to lose. Not the same man I was ten years ago. (I'd probably be dead if I was). I'm not as lonely and deeply depressed as I was then.

I decided not to reactivate the account. Why? To be honest I didn't want to open Pandora's Box. I'll just try sticking to family who I love and cherish. And fishing, football and rum - rum is immense.

That love affair started in Jamaica. The first time we went to Half Moon Beach - Sitting on my friend's beach sinking Appleton in utterly idyllic surroundings. Not sure if I've ever been more relaxed.

Then there was the trip to Appleton Estate Distillery. They start with serving rum punch. My wife hates rum; I think I had six before we started. I was on a Caribbean island, beautiful woman by my side and rum in abundance - glorious.

At the end they had every type of rum they produce in one room - twenty minutes of unlimited tasting. Me? I headed straight for their most expensive; and finest vintage - and listened to their tasting official while he poured drinks and explained more of the islands' history. You can drink plenty of rum in twenty minutes. I was blasted, and blissfully happy, when I left. Where was my wife you might me thinking? The rum hater... In the gift shop buying me rum! I know. Surely one of the luckiest men alive....

SATURDAY 25 FEBRUARY
00.50AM

I ended up meeting my dad for a pint. It's always nice. Beforehand we went to the Shepherd Neame shop to buy ale. As I tried to load it into the car I dropped a case - glass every-where – what an idiot.

Not the first time I've done this. Years ago, I got a taxi to a lake near my house. I was in a bad place. Unloading my fishing gear; I dropped a bottle of vodka in the road. Fucking thing smashed everywhere. I absolutely stank. I was livid, and highly flammable. It was one of those periods of time when nothing went right.

I kept Bubba until a few minutes ago. My wife was tired, emotional and needed a rest. Am I tired? I'm passed caring. Not sure anyone else is bothered either.

SUNDAY 26 FEBRUARY
10.20PM

Illness - it's everywhere. My wife had to go to minor injuries due to another infection. She'll be back at the doctor tomorrow.

I took our eldest out for the afternoon in not the best weather. We went to a nice pub up the road. With a big sheltered garden. What followed was a beer and two hours of wind-swept hide-and-seek, football and bundles. We were both exhausted when we left. When we got home it was straight into the PJ's.

Bubba was very unsettled - took me ages to get her down. I sent Mummy to bed as soon as our eldest was down.

Back to work Tuesday – can't wait…

9.00AM

My IBS has flared up. Not taken my inhaler for ages. I'm drinking too much caffeine. I feel sick. My headache is never ending. I'm just a mess.

An hour after I took Bubba up, out eldest kicked off, wouldn't sleep. At about half two I gave up. We both went down on the sofa. She eventually went to sleep just before four o'clock.

7.45PM

I'm tired and demotivated. At least I've only got a three-day week. Tomorrow is going to be awful. I'm thirty-eight in a week. Time for my mid-life thing? Or is that fifty now? I'm going to have a think about this over the next few days. It won't be all smiles - far from it. It won't be dull though.

Alexis,

Thank you sincerely for all your emotional support and intellectual input from day one. When I was feeling so down and self-conscious at the start, and terrified of being ridiculed and seen as a failure, you've just been you. You always said you were always only at the other end of the phone, even though you were thousands of miles away. Just that alone made me feel like I had a human value, at times when I thought I was worthless - it's a debt I'll never be able to repay — it doesn't have monetary value.

Love from Blighty,

Steve x

From Zero to...

Thirty-eight years old, about half of my life
Two amazing children, a beautiful wife,

But as mortality bites, a sad realisation,
I've still not found my life's vocation

So many jobs, never a career,
Being a failure, my biggest fear,

It's all my own fault; the feelings of pain,
An awful role model, indescribable shame

With my life I'm now trying to do something worthwhile,
To get myself off the bottom of the pile

My mantra is now just to give it my best,
From now 'til the day I'm laid to rest

Needed a decent night sleep and got it. Just. My head still aches. My joints ache. Dark clouds building. It's a mind-set thing. I didn't have my head on. It was full of barriers, negativity, obstacles, resistance. I'm moody.

My irrationality has returned. I looked in the mirror and hate my appearance. Spoke to my wife about my body dysmorphia. She's known about this for a while. It's bizarre. I hate looking in the mirror. And when I do I refuse to see what's there. Or just can't see it. I can't explain it.

Body Dysmorphic Disorder

Body dysmorphic disorder (BDD) is an anxiety disorder related to body image. If you have BDD, these obsessions and behaviours cause emotional distress and have a significant impact on your ability to carry on with your day-to-day life. (Source: Mind website)

She tries to help by buying me clothes that suit my shape and skin tone and hair colour - being as supportive and understanding as she can. She said she knows it's just another challenge I face. And she's never judged me. Despite how my conditions and bad behaviour have affected her.

My eldest has started waking up our Little Bubba every time she goes to sleep. Competing for attention; being disruptive. Also keeping my eye on my wife - she can't get burned out. I need to be supporting her all day, every day. But it's more than having to, it's wanting to, right?

FOUR. BIRTHDAY, BOOZE AND BAD DREAMS

WEDNESDAY 1 MARCH
00.45AM

Now crashed on the sofa; watching a documentary about supermassive black holes. It's fascinating. I love the subject, and Stephen Hawking, he's a genius. Black holes grow by consuming stars, rocks, debris and space dust. It's almost incomprehensible. Apparently in five billion years, our galaxy will merge with another, Andromeda. And the black holes at the centre of both galaxies will merge and destroy both - the concept of oblivion again. Five billion years. We won't even be on earth then. In a couple of hundred years we'll have ruined it... My mind is racing out of control. When I get like this I start getting hot and shaking.

Out Friday for birthday drinks. I suggested my wife thinks about going out one evening with her friends. She burst into tears. Told me she's not ready to go out. I'm worried about her. I just want her to be happy.

I've been up for the last hour with our eldest. Nightmares and a bit lip.

She's finally gone down I think...

I've just looked in the mirror - I'm ugly, unattractive; morose.

THURSDAY 2 MARCH
9.15PM

Our eldest had nightmares again. Night was rubbish. Here's the irony. My other two ladies got loads of sleep. My wife had an argument with our eldest. Who said she didn't like Bubba anymore. I came home and had a proper talk with our eldest; talked to her like an adult. For a while I was the only person in the room not crying. But I was crying inside, sobbing.

I bought my wife a beautiful Birthday/Mother's Day present. It's a framed collage of photos I've taken since Bubba was born.

Nan has her oncology appointment tomorrow. It's always on my mind. How my dad sleeps I'll never know. Maybe he doesn't…

FRIDAY 3 MARCH
01.10AM

I had a great evening. And feel battered. I chilled out in a quiet boozer in town for half an hour before meeting some close friends at our local kebab restaurant. It's owned by the dad of one of my oldest friends. Both were working tonight. The food is always excellent. I love the atmosphere. It's warm and friendly; unpretentious and relaxed.

We chatted for ages and had a good catch up. Red wine accompanied the meal. Large cognacs ended it. We were also given bottles of red as a gift. My friend and his dad are both gentlemen and genuinely nice people. They deserve all their success.

It reminded me of my fun times in the trade. Some of my happiest times were when I was working as a wine waiter in France. I was young, free, and loving life. I took pride in serving drinks. For weeks I practised pouring single and double shots free-hand into shot glasses - until I got it spot on. Our customers loved the way I mixed drinks, and the fact I spoke French. I'm not sure I've ever had as much self-confidence as I did then. I pulled French women with ease. I felt immense. Now I spend most of my time battling with feeling a complete and total failure - crazy how times change.

SATURDAY 4 MARCH
8.30PM

I woke up on the sofa. Fully dressed; money in every pocket - mouth like a camels' posterior; head absolutely pounding.

Had some of my wife's family for lunch - I looked after our eldest and sorted the kitchen. It's important she has quality family time.

Our eldest was exhausted from about mid-afternoon. She wanted to sleep downstairs, because she does at Nanny and Grandad's house. I told her no. She went ape. I had to ring my dad straight away. If she stays there she must sleep in a bed.

There can't be mixed messages. She's too clever. She needs firm, consistent, but loving parenting.

We're out for lunch tomorrow. I'm really looking forward to it. Mental health is okay. Looking back on the last year I can't believe so much has happened.

SUNDAY 5 MARCH
8.12PM

I can't be more than ten feet from the bog.

Lunch with my parents was nice. My ladies were on good form. It was nice getting out as a family.

Having a glass of rum and relaxing - before the wake-ups start, and contemplating being thirty-eight tomorrow. It's just a number, right? Or is it? Realistically, I'm half way through my life. Seventy-six is a decent knock. It's scary; the older you get. The more you value everything. You change the way you think - take less risks.

But it's also exciting. Got a young family? Your life is full of love and chaos. And you can enjoy watching your children grow up. Single? You can travel. Pursue your dream job. Emigrate. What's the most important thing? I'd say having no regrets. So far, I've done okay. Travelled; studied and lived abroad. Then ran a business. Faced addictions but partied like a rock star. Settled down, and now have a family. And then there's the mania, mental health and the suicide stuff, my dark side.

Tomorrow my eldest is getting her second gym badge. I'm not working, so can go watch her - can't wait.

To the second half of my life - I say bring it on. I'm ready...

MY BIRTHDAY
7.55PM

What a lovely family day and one massive accident. Fell asleep on the sofa after my girls bundled me and opened my presents. Coming into spring/summer? I get loads of jumpers. Maybe it's because I'm so fat? Shirts barely fit me anymore.

The money my parents agreed to lend me didn't hit my account. Why? I'd transposed two numbers in the account number. What an idiot. If it had been an active account, we'd have struggled to get it back. Luckily Mum did. So, I ran from the gym class to the bank to meet her. Then had to run back - another gauge my mental health still seems to be okay. Had I been in a bad way, I would've spiralled, probably breaking down. Today I managed to keep it together. Just.

Made it back in time for her presentation; I was so proud. We blew kisses at each-other.

I'll never forget my thirty-eighth birthday - my first as a father of two. I feel truly blessed.

TUESDAY 7 MARCH
8.40PM

I'm relatively calm. Work is so busy though. You can see, feel and hear the strain. A lot of people are worried. Some are working from home at weekends - unpaid. Not me. I've been there before. It's not healthy. And I don't need any other external issues impacting me. I have enough on my plate already.

WEDNESDAY 8 MARCH
10.00PM

Bad day at work... Dad picked me up and asked me to visit Nan with Bubba. She has another appointment next week. Dad says it won't be good news. I asked if this means she's now reduced to pain relief - in other words dying. My dad said yes under his breath. It probably sounded insensitive. But if I don't know what's going on, I don't know how I can help and support him. We're grown men. And you want to help however you can, right?

Started watching the Barcelona vs PSG game - (Non-football fans... Please indulge me. Or turn the page! I'm not proud. I don't want to bore you!) They pulled off one of the greatest comebacks in the history of European football by winning six-one at home after losing the first leg four-nil. Not the greatest comeback though...

It started on Tuesday 3 May 2005. My dear pal and I watched the Liverpool vs Chelsea European Cup semi-final second leg in a Canterbury boozer. As the final whistle blew sealing Liverpool's progression to the final he told me I had to go to the game. Drunk; I accepted the challenge. Next day I bought my match ticket - £450. Then I tried to book a flight - I could only fly to Bulgaria - another £350. My ticket was in the

Milan end. I was separated from everyone. I left my bags in the minibus - never saw them again. Luckily, I took my passport, money, phone and travel docs into the game with me.

When Shevchenko missed his penalty? Oh my...The stadium was Euphoric. Liverpool had won The European Cup for the fifth time. I stumbled out the stadium - then got put on my arse by a bus with no wing mirrors and dubious lights. When the plane landed back in London I went straight to Lords for a day of test cricket and Pimm's - I was a booze infused shambles - but absolutely buzzing.

There is still so much more to this story. But that's another book. It was, though, the best trip ever.

THURSDAY 9 MARCH
6.20PM

Burnt myself out today before work - had a whip round the house. I got to work on time, but my head wasn't in it. We're so busy. I know I've probably wound some people up. I can't control my paranoia. I think it's something I have or haven't done, which is probably nonsense. It's also extremely self-centred. It looks like I think the world revolves around me. What about the flip-side? Well, when people are happy; I never think it's because of something I've done; or said.

First time in ages I got the bus. At the bus stop everyone was on their phones. You can leave the house and never feel lonely. I'm the reverse - battling with loneliness when surrounded by people. It's hard to describe. I wouldn't wish these feelings on anyone. I regularly feel lonely at work - my coping mechanism? I just focus on my job. And ride it out or send a text to my wife or a friend. It's just part of my life now.

Need to see Nan this weekend. I promised Dad.

FRIDAY 10 MARCH
8.25PM

Today can just fuck off. And not come back.

It started lovely - loads done at home. My eldest went to nursery good as gold. Went to Nan's, she said it was lovely to meet our Little Bubba. And it was worth the wait. I nearly cried. It reminded me of The Royle Family episode 'The Queen of Sheba'. Nanna said the same thing when she met little baby Norma. Nanna died days later...

Anyway, Nan had a long cuddle. I took some lovely photos - and kept my promise to Dad.

Half way home we heard a clunk. Thought the exhaust pipe had fallen off. No chance - a busted flywheel and a £1200 bill.

Got home and tried to help our eldest in the toilet. I swung my arm round full pelt - full weight behind it. I smacked my elbow into the wall and door frame - absolute agony. She laughed.

At her bedtime I was still in agony. Just as I handed Bubba back to Mummy she covered me in warm, lumpy sick. What a hat-trick. Had I been given a match ball it would have undoubtedly been drilled right into my testicles...

Taking her to bed was a nightmare. She didn't stop talking.

After twenty minutes. I just burst out laughing - couldn't help it. It was either that or burst into tears. It could have gone either way.

The worst day I've had for some time. I might even stay up until 12.01. Just so I can give it the finger...

SATURDAY 11 MARCH
7.24PM

I'm worried about my wife. She is very tired and emotional. I've told all three of our parents. I need help. To make sure she doesn't regress. We all love her dearly. And need to keep an eye on her. I want to look after her - to protect her.

Me? My head's not right. I can feel the imbalance. I'm not in control. I can't sleep either. Mind racing, skin hot, body twitching.

SUNDAY 12 MARCH
8.50PM

Today was a grind. For the third night running I barely slept. My problem is not being able to sleep until late. Then when one of the girls wakes... I'm still wide awake after they're long gone.

Felt sick all morning. Thumping head - limbs heavy. I fell asleep twice sitting up on the sofa. I was holding Bubba both times - lucky I didn't drop her. I was proper snappy too; wasn't right. So much so I had to tell my wife. She didn't deserve it.

I had no excuse. I was out of order.

I didn't want to go out but had to go to my mother-in-law's for lunch. I did not feel sociable. Conversation was a struggle. The paranoia was so painful; so debilitating. The children played well though and my wife had a nice time. And everyone was fussing over our Little Bubba. She's lucky to have such a loving family around her.

I looked in the mirror just now. It was horrible. My body shape is so unattractive. It's nasty. My wife will end up leaving me. Not that I'm saying she's unfaithful. But I think it won't be long until she just doesn't find me physically attractive anymore. And it scares me. It's my own fault. I couldn't blame her. Looking like I do now. I imagine most women are repulsed by me. Who knows? She might already feel that way. And it makes me feel worthless.

MONDAY 13 MARCH
8.25PM

Our eldest was troubled last night - having very bad dreams. I couldn't take any more. I woke up at six o'clock after about two hours sleep. I didn't go to work. I couldn't face it, or people.

The house is going through a bit of a rough patch. It's hard. My ladies have doctor's appointments this week and next. And we have no car, or money.

We're honest hardworking people. We don't want much. Yet some of the 'luck' we have is truly abysmal. It feels like a test. How much can we take?

Totally forgot about everything coming up:

- Easter egg hunt
- Mother's Day
- Our fifth Wedding Anniversary
- My wife's Birthday

I've currently only bought her one big present. I need to get a couple more things if I can.

Out Little Bubba is six weeks old on Thursday – time really does fly doesn't it? Our parents adore her. (But to be fair they're the same with our eldest.) She'll be crawling soon. Then God help us.

I need to start looking for other jobs. I've not discussed this with my wife properly. We need to get through this rough patch - before I load our plates with the next course of gourmet manure.

For now, it's just for me. But we've all worked in jobs where we've been insecure and/or unhappy, haven't we? Some of us still are. We get on with it don't we? And probably just have a whinge down the boozer with the lads. Alcohol is a depressant. That's why so many people end up a mess at the end of a night, fights happen, and people cry. It's one of the most dangerous, addictive drugs on earth.

But I like it.

My mental health has been deteriorating for three days. My head is rushing, my mind's darting everywhere. And it's dark.

How poorly is Nan? Will she be able to have treatment? The stutter appointment is tomorrow. What are they going to say? Will *she* need treatment? Is my wife okay? She's not been right since she came home from hospital (in my opinion anyway). The car is a nightmare. What's going to happen to my job? Do I fit in there? Do they want me there? So much uncertainty - so few answers. So unstable; or is that just me?

Three days ago, a mirror fell on our stairs. Not put it back up or looked in it since. It coincided almost exactly with my mental health decline. A couple of my colleagues told me I looked bad today. I went to the toilet – and forced myself to look in the mirror - they weren't wrong.

I told one of my bosses. Better I do than someone else. I don't want anyone presuming anything. I said I don't want it to be a big thing. I'm simply providing an information update. I'm happy to talk. But I hate feeling I need to; it feels insincere.

Got home; greeted by huge running hugs - such a lovely thing to come home to. Everyone looked okay - apart from me...

The house looked tidy, my wife, beautiful. I don't know how she does it. She's amazing.

So is our eldest. One of her favourite things is yoga. I said we'd start doing it together after I finish work. Bedtime stories are currently Thomas the Tank Engine. She was asleep before I'd finished. Tucked her in; peck on the cheek. And I left the room - another day older. I'll be forty in the blink of an eye.

WEDNESDAY 15 MARCH
8.30PM

But she was up most of the night. Wanted nothing; but everything. She's speaking so well - even though her stutter is bad. But I never feel like I really know what she's thinking; what she wants and needs. Still feels like guesswork. She's three. I'm not sure it should be.

Yes sir, speech therapy on the NHS? You'll be on the waiting list for a year. Our GP advised us to go private. Says it all doesn't it?

Work was weird. Felt calmer, but my paranoia was bad. Every time I looked up and saw someone laughing I immediately assumed it was at my expense. Later in the day I was manic – pre-occupied with my eldest's problems. I felt guilty. Sick. So twitchy.

I need a shave. I'm starting to look like Peter Sutcliffe again.

THURSDAY 16 MARCH
11.00PM

Flat out today. My absence management review went okay. Review period extended for another three months. Told them about my lapse - not sure how it was received. My condensed hours will be reviewed in April. I'll be gutted if they're stopped.

Nan was found this morning in her living room - freezing cold. She had a hospital appointment this afternoon. My uncle took her there.

FRIDAY 17 MARCH
20.39PM

In the afternoon we went out for an hour as a family. By the end of the afternoon I was tired; losing patience and tolerance.

Nan had two blasts of Chemo yesterday - today an ECG. The heart and vital signs check. Can't gauge how my dad's feeling. He's not saying much. We're going for a beer tomorrow though so should get a better idea then.

I desperately need a hair-cut. I look like a hobo.

SATURDAY 18 MARCH
8.10PM

Our eldest slept through. I didn't; so, it meant nothing to me. I was so pleased for her though.

I had arranged to meet my dad for a beer, right? My penance was cleaning out both fridges; putting the shopping away and hoovering beforehand.

I still felt guilty when I left. It's years since I went one day without feel guilty about something. Think I've given up trying to resolve this - I just accept and manage it. I feel I've got the co-dependency under control. I'm past solely doing things to please others. That's part of the reason I've made progress in the last nine months.

Co-dependency is typically discussed in the context of substance use, where one person is abusing the substance, and he or she depends on the other person to supply money, food, or shelter. But co-dependency is much broader than that.

Says Jonathan Becker, DO, assistant professor of clinical psychiatry at Vanderbilt University in Nashville, Tennessee.

Co-dependency can be defined as any relationship in which two people become so invested in each other that they can't function independently anymore. Your mood, happiness, and identity are defined by the other person. (Source: Everyday Health website)

Nice to see my parents; I sank a few Hurlimann. We talked family. I'm realising that if this book is ever published people might be upset by some of it... But the truth sometimes hurts right...? Something else I can feel guilty about.

Our eldest scooted to Sainsbury without her helmet. I forgot it. Mummy was not impressed. I could have lied and said I took it. But told the truth and felt like I was failing as a parent. She knows her left and right now, so we've started doing the green cross code. Her stutter was very bad; I must email the therapist. And sort out the car money.

It's Saturday night, so what am I doing? Flopped on the floor; football on the box. Writing this on my phone - drink? Rum over ice... The house is silent.

Our eldest was up at quarter to four; ready to go full throttle. It's lovely – but so hard early in the morning. She just can't understand why everyone else isn't up. And wants to wake them!

My insomnia was bad, so I ended up watching the whole series of This Is England '86. And it's brilliant.

Finally got my hair cut - I can't believe I walked around looking like that. What must people have thought? Some appalled. Some concerned. Some amused. Some bemused.

Been watching Bottom – Rik Mayall was a genius. He was a beautiful and magnetic individual. Three years now since he died; like my grandad. That's why memories are so important.

Death plays a huge part in our lives. And everybody embraces it with varying levels of acceptance, distance and denial. My fixation started when I was about eight or nine. I was walking back from the park near my house and a black hearse drove slowly past me. It looked massive; intimidating. In flowers was written 'Daddy' on the side. I stood in the middle of the road. Watching it glide away from me. For years that's all I thought about. And often still do… What happens next? Is that the end? I thought about my family and when I'd lose them. I've often wished I died young because it's easier than living until an old age and losing everyone around you. My selfish side again. I never told anyone about that until now.

Dark circles

Oblivion the start; we enter the world,
Screaming aloud, but never a word,

Rites of passage, we hurtle through life
Through pain and delight, trouble and strife,

When confronted with questions like 'why are we here?'
'What's the meaning of life, what should we fear?

So many worried about their last breath
Unable to cope with the concept of death,

Looking back on our time, hoping to smile
Does it flash before us, just for a while?

All we can hope for, is reincarnation,
As we exit the world, back into oblivion

Now I'm probably more worried about how I'll be remembered. Will there be anyone at my funeral? Will my life have been worth celebrating? And mourning?

Paranoid even in death... Mental isn't it. I sound like a fruitcake. More fruit than cake.

MONDAY 20 MARCH
8.18PM

Didn't get shot - but had a dream about my wife running off with one of the ladies I work with. Just remember being in a café; then them getting up from a table holding hands and not even looking back. Then my eyes opened scanning around; my head spinning. Even though I knew where I was. Think I'd rather get shot. My eldest slept through. She always does when I don't.

The girls are poorly again. Nearly didn't go to work. My wife made me; even though she looked poorly. Of course, I felt guilty... I just tried not to think about it.

No matter how you live your life, good or bad, every life ends in the same way. The heart stops beating. The body goes cold. Death row has always fascinated me. As have the people on it. But something perplexes me. People who are executed have a quick, pain-free death. Invariably their victims don't.

I think this is a big part of religion - people are scared by death. And the unknown that awaits. So, belief in heaven makes transition easier. I personally don't believe in any of it. Procreation raises life from nothing. Death returns it to nothing. It's the cycle of life.

I'm absolutely all over the place. My head is speeding.

Three days to the fishing trip.

TUESDAY 21 MARCH
7.00AM

Had to get the train - left early and arrived in plenty of time. Guess what? It's broken down. And the signalling is failing. We're going nowhere. The masses are restless.

It's how my life is going right now.

If I cracked an egg it'd have no yolk.

The girls are really bonding well. It's amazing to be a part of. Although I'm not around as much as I want to be. Our eldest is a caring, loving big sister. Time's elapsing so fast. I wish it would slow down.

WEDNESDAY 22 MARCH
9.10PM

I was in the kitchen for an hour before work. Scrambled head; still not sorted out the speech therapist yet. My wife seems to be okay. I'm up and down. Don't know why my paranoia won't shift. I'm over-analysing everything. When I say something I think; did the person take it as it was meant? Have I offended someone? Do people like me? I feel like I stick out like a sore thumb. Every interaction is a struggle.

I got home to the usual; love and mayhem. But I was not feeling myself. It's making my head, shoulders and heart heavy.

THURSDAY 23 MARCH
8.30PM

I sat sweating in the corner of the living room all last night. Hot but freezing and wrapped in a blanket. Sweating and hallucinating. Savage chest pains. I went to work.

I was very low all day. Off with everyone; impatient with residents. Not my style, not me. I didn't even work for the last hour of the day.

Still haven't sorted our eldest a therapist.

SATURDAY 25 MARCH
LATE

I've been sweating for two days solid - still a fat twat though.

SUNDAY 26 MARCH 9.35PM
THE FISHING TRIP/MOTHER'S DAY

Left the house Friday morning; didn't even say goodbye to my ladies. No surprise I was pulled about it. It takes two minutes to say goodbye. And dish out some hugs – shameful, selfish parenting.

Went with two old friends which was fun - the lake wasn't though. It was a scabby hole in the ground. Most people started drinking about 11.00am. I was a bit later I think. The evening was a rum fest. One of the guys had a proper coal smoker. After about eight hours drinking we had a shoulder of lamb. We ate like kings. Acted like twats. Perfect.

I don't remember walking back to my tent.

I had a huge hangover Saturday morning - and was already missing my ladies and home. I felt like I was failing as an angler, husband and dad. Our little Bubba was born weeks ago. And I wasn't at home. I also felt like I was suffocating. I needed my own space but couldn't get it - you can't on a social. I was supposed to be convalescing. And no; alcohol doesn't help but it's my choice. I drink and need to manage the effects and outcomes. I'm a grown man.

Not a little boy.

By the time I got up people were already on the beer. I tentatively sipped Stella for the afternoon. But crashed out by eight o'clock, I needed some space and to avoid more heavy drinking.

Packing up was dreadful. No fish and not enough sleep. Alcohol and meat sweats – smelling rank. The journey back wasn't fun either - just the sense everyone'd had enough. Back at home everyone was tired. Not really the environment I wanted to walk back into. But it's family life; and fatherhood... What was I expecting, a rest? Seriously! It's embarrassing to admit. (But I'm not backing down. You're seeing and reading everything I'm going through. I said you can judge me. I stand by that).

My mum loved her presents and loved having our eldest for the weekend.

My wife loved the personalised photo frame.

Bubba's growing by the day and smiling now. It's the most beautiful thing. You normally get one after you've fed her. And she's burped.

Our eldest could be a child model. Not that we'd push her into anything. She can make her own decisions under guidance - when she's old enough. That's why I'm not on social media. I don't think it's fair children have a footprint without even knowing. But it's also a very personal, parenting decision. And everyone feels very differently. What if I did? And they my girls got to the age of seven and said 'Why have you done that? I don't like it'. Then I'm screwed? And I see the irony about writing this book and including them. Ultimately my hope is that it will help them understand me and feel closer to me. And if they ever experience any issues they know they'll be able to come to me, and that I'll understand.

MONDAY 27 MARCH

21.22PM

I saw a photo of myself with some friends in the pub. I looked disgusting; obese. It made me want to cry. I wanted to make myself sick. But I don't want a new addiction.

I was bullied at school, particularly secondary because of my size. Have you been through it? Then you'll know how I felt. And still feel. Especially as a bloke, we're just expected to brush it off as banter. That's utter crap. And if you were one of those people who bullied others (which I also did). Here's how you made them feel. Not nice is it?

I had one or two girlfriends at school. I had no self-confidence. I drank heavily at parties, so I could distance myself from the failure I felt I was becoming.

When my first marriage was breaking down, suicide was something I spent months contemplating. Don't remember how many pills I took that night with the litre of vodka.

I moved back home and threw myself into exercise. Running every night and following extreme portion control. No booze. Not even skin on chicken. Comfort in a new *healthy* addiction.

Suicide is still a taboo subject. In 2016, The Office for national Statistics published Statistics Bulletin: Suicides in Great Britain: 2016 registrations which stated of the 5,668 suicides registered in 2016, there were 4,287 male and 1,381, female… (Source: ONS website.)

This is an even larger than the number that I was expecting. And shows the enormity of both the size of the problem, and the challenge our society faces to stop so many people taking their lives every year.

I dropped weight steadily and started going to clubs. (Which I never did as a fat teenager - it was just another environment for me to experience rejection). I got loads of women and barely had to try. Physically I was in great shape. Mentally and emotionally I was at rock bottom. But the ladies didn't care. It just shows how shallow, superficial, and brutal society can be. After about six weeks of that I was lucky enough to meet my current wife. Not at a club either. I was a total prick during that period. She'd not have looked at me twice if she'd met me then.

It's no exaggeration to say she saved my life - and has been helping me rebuild it since that day; often without even knowing. That's why I want to do everything I possibly can for her.

Mad, sad, dysfunctional dad…

TUESDAY 28 MARCH
8.35PM

I'm watching a documentary about solitary confinement at Ohio State Prison. That's a good way of describing how my mental state is currently - lonely, separated, confined, boxed in - nowhere to go and no escape. Nowhere to turn; and no options.

A couple of people could see I wasn't right. I couldn't hide it today.

And didn't have the energy to try and hide it.

Bubba has started smiling. In the morning she beams. It makes me smile, however I'm feeling.

Our eldest is very challenging. In the kitchen she'll move a chair, so she can reach high shelves or the top of the fridge. She can smell lies a mile off. She manipulates me; especially at bedtime. But I don't want her to start associating bedtime with unhappiness. It needs to be associated with warmth and love. Her stutter seems to have lessened. Still haven't sorted a therapist. Why? I don't know. I have no excuse. I'm a bad dad.

Eyes down (but no bingo)

Eye contact, it's such a simple art,
Inability to do it, tears me apart

Sitting in a bar, looking at the table,
Just another example of being unstable

People watching is supposed to be fun
Can't hold my head up, just want to run,

Can't look in mirrors, afraid of what's there
No love for myself; it's never been there...

WEDNESDAY 29 MARCH
6.50AM

Our eldest barely slept last night. By four o'clock I lost my patience. Felt so guilty. I'm going to the doctor again on Friday. Suicidal thoughts are creeping back in. It's the first time since I started therapy. I can't control my mind. Just don't feel like smiling. I'll have to put on a happy face today. I said I'd never do it again. But I can't stand the thought of people fussing over me.

I didn't say goodbye to anyone as I left. I closed the front door in silence as I left.

The Abyss

Dark's not just a colour, it is a mood
In a room full of friends, my silence is rude

So many bad thoughts swamping my head
Someone talking to me; fills me with dread

I've nothing to say, I just think I'm boring
Paranoia takes hold, the voices are waring

The anguish is real, a head full of fear,
Time and again, hiding with beer

Company not, but conversation I miss
This is the reality, of The Abyss.

THURSDAY 30 MARCH
8.53PM

Our eldest slept through last night. The girls are feeling better. Me? I'm having horrendous dreams again. This time I made a pass at one of the ladies from work. Guess what? I got rejected... Even in them I'm a failure!

I did more reading. Apparently, this signifies a lack of self-worth. And feeling alienated. As well as low self-confidence - and fears manifesting in dreams.

I wrote a text to my wife about how I was feeling. But deleted it, never sent it. Why? Maybe I was worried about the reply? Scared I'd worry her? Maybe I didn't want her to think I was struggling again - that I'm a fat failure.

I didn't start taking my drops like I told her I would. I'm wary of the mania. As low as I felt yesterday, today I was up; energised. People are starting to see it. Maybe even feel it. Who knows?

When I came home my wife looked tired. The girls were okay. Things seem to be returning to normal. I made her take a little bit of down time – I must take more of the strain.

My eldest's been invited to another party. I'm so proud of her. She's my princess.

FRIDAY 31 MARCH 2017
11.24PM

It was a good night. But my head won't shift.

I had some more cuddle time with Bubba today with nobody around. She has such a beautiful, gummy grin. Took a few snaps. My phone is now my life. It's irreplaceable, unlike me.

We went to a local wildlife park – our eldest met a nice little girl. And they played all afternoon. She looked so happy until she stacked it. She needs covering in bubble-wrap.

Now she's grumbling…

Phew, she's gone back off. Her bedtime routine is *still* shot to pieces - as is my patience.

FIVE. RUM-DRUNK AND ALONE

SATURDAY 1 APRIL
SOMETIME AFTER MIDNIGHT

What a manic day... Massive family day - I'm rum drunk. Started as a family day - then a call from my dad; my nan is in hospital. Nobody is saying anything. But I've been here before with my grandad. I know what comes next, and I'm sick of it. I can't even be bothered to process all this, let alone write.

SUNDAY 2 APRIL
9.20PM

Reading last night's entry - only hazy memories of writing it... Rum saw to that. A few things I omitted.

I spent the afternoon with our eldest and I taught her about the weather. She now knows that when the sun goes behind the cloud it gets dark and cold. That wind blows the clouds. And when clouds are stormy rain comes. Amazing; she's incredible.

This morning I peeled myself off the sofa. First boot fair of the year. Still felt like guff at lunchtime. Bubba fed every hour today. Must be a growth spurt, it's ridiculous. But it meant I got loads of cuddles.

Nan's home; and nobody really seems to know anything.

MONDAY 3 APRIL
9.20PM

Our eldest was seriously unhappy last night; screaming. (It's a miracle my other two ladies didn't wake.) She needed lots of cuddles. And she got them.

Work was utterly uninteresting.

Our eldest seems a bit happier in herself. Stutter was a little better. But I'm different around her. Listening more and speaking less; being more patient. Bubba's now in her big girl crib.

I'm finding it hard to feel motivated by anything. I'm totally disinterested and constantly tired. Need to visit my nan. Still don't know what's going on.

When I was young I used to sit in her front garden drawing landscape pictures on the back of old wallpaper rolls; mainly of the pub and nearby houses. I spent hours there. The end-product was always average. But she used to bring me tea and cake. And tell me how brilliant I was. Such happy memories – making me smile as a write. And cry too.

Our eldest slept through again. The bedtime routine is developing.

Work was a little better. I still wonder what the point is. But I try and focus on helping people as much as I can. I think if I wasn't so far along our absence management procedure I'd have taken a couple of days in the last month. I'm always so paranoid when I'm off. How will this affect my job? When will my next meeting with HR be? How long will they put up with me? And I end up returning to work before I'm well enough to. So, I'm always starting from a bad place. Currently mania and paranoia are really affecting me.

Mania

Mania is a feeling of being extremely 'high', with lots of energy and enthusiasm. It's different from a normal good mood, because the feelings are very intense or go on for a long time. Mania can appear as part of bipolar disorder, or on its own. Hypomania is a milder form of mania (Source: Young Minds website)

Everyone is tired. It won't shift. I've nothing in the tank by the time I get home. I feel guilty for feeling tired - even looking tired.

Washing has finished - got to get the stuff out. Life's relentless, so is this book - but for you hopefully in a good way. You've got to know how I feel if you're going to connect with me.

Oh no… It's our Wedding Anniversary on Thursday; no

time to get a present. I bought the ring. But I need to buy a card and some flowers. It's her birthday in eleven days too. Mum's birthday Friday - like I said; *relentless*.

And expensive.

WEDNESDAY 5 APRIL
9.00PM

Relentless is right – our eldest was wild again. She woke at 1.00am. What time did she resettle? Half past three. I arrived at work feeling empty. Mental health isn't too bad. But paranoia is consuming me.

Another day staring at a computer screen barely talking to anyone. I always have lunch on my own. I reckon people think I'm weird or rude. Writing is my solace.

Our eldest is wild again. It's going to be a very, very long night. Another one will break me.

Bubba had her first jabs today and was so cuddly this evening.

Dad wasn't right today. Then I found out why. Monday is the third anniversary of his dad's (my grandad's) death.

Relentless

THURSDAY 6 APRIL
6.00AM

I thought our wedding anniversary was today. It was Tuesday… How could I forget?

I hate myself… I want to rip my toenails off.

The hate I felt towards myself yesterday has become disdain and loathing. It won't go away. I don't feel I deserve anyone or anything.

My wife does absolutely everything for this family. She's cared for Bubba for the last two days since her jabs. She's even been making me lunch. It feels like she's looking after me too. How can that be right?

Everyone in the house is poorly. It's a revolving door of illness. Our eldest has started free nursery. You'd think I'd be delighted? No; for two reasons. She's now off on a Friday, which means she misses yoga; her favourite activity. And I no longer get a break for half a day. I hate reading how selfish this make me look and sound. But I must be honest. No matter how much I hate the feelings it generates.

Mum's birthday tomorrow. Guess who chose and paid for her present?

FRIDAY 7 APRIL - MUM'S BIRTHDAY

9.00PM

My head's pounding. Went to go to the shops today; couldn't find my wallet. Looks like I left it on the train last night. I had to cancel my bank cards, indescribably furious.

While dad and I were altering the crib, I lost the alum key - a total mind-blank. And did it twice with my phone. When I was signed off this was one of my scariest symptoms; having no recall. I've been told by my doctor and therapist memory blackouts aren't uncommon for someone with mental health problems like mine. It's still petrifying.

My mum enjoyed her tea party. My ladies made an awesome cake and the weather was beautiful. Me? I fell asleep on the sofa. What a prick. She loved her presents though.

Our eldest is crying again. I wish she wasn't.

10.00PM

She's been crying for the last twenty minutes. I've been in to her twice already. If I was upstairs the whole house would be awake. Every time I sit down she cries. I honestly don't know what to do. Our minds and bodies need time to heal

10.45PM

And this is how it ends. After some comforting she passed out. I'm left on the sofa - with just the television and my insomnia for company. It's dark, I'm wired and alone; tired, and sad. I don't often actually say I feel sad.

Insomnia

Insomnia is difficulty getting to sleep or staying asleep for long enough to feel refreshed the next morning. Persistent insomnia can have a significant impact on your quality of life. It can limit what you're able to do during the day, affect your mood, and lead to relationship problems with friends, family and colleagues (Source: NHS Scotland website)

SATURDAY 8 APRIL
10.45PM

My life is organised chaos; my mind is just chaos.

Our eldest had a party, and we arrived before the parents! She had a lovely time. I just watched her on the trampoline for the first part. Far better balance than I ever had. She keeps talking about her best friend, so we managed to find her parents; invited her to our Easter egg hunt.

I was drinking coffee again - against my better judgement and therapists' advice – bad old habits, but familiar comforts.

Bubba's grabbing everything. Her favourite is my arm-hair. I've started calling her *My Beamer* - because of her smile.

I've had a few glasses of wine. It still isn't calming the chaos in my head. Maybe ketamine would do it... It seems to work for people coming down off heroin, and horses.

SUNDAY 9 APRIL
6.50PM

The hottest day of the year so far and my hangover was huge.

It took me a while to get my bearings. It's the third anniversary of my grandad's passing. We went to the boot fair. As usual, I chased our eldest around (sweating booze) while my wife had some down time and did some browsing.

I must've looked and smelled awful. Popped into my parents; my sister was arguing with them, and I lost it. Hangovers shorten people's patience and tolerance. I don't think our eldest will be staying there for a while. Her stutter is still improving. I won't let anything affect her. Maybe I overreacted. But your gut instinct is normally right.

Mum and dad went to London for the Thames River cruise my wife bought them. No guilt there!

We headed to the farm near my nan's house. It has a nice miniature steam railway that goes on a loop through the orchards. I chilled with Bubba. It's important my wife has as much quality time with our eldest as possible.

I'm exhausted, sweaty, grumpy and dehydrated. Wish I'd stayed off from the grape juice last night.

MONDAY 10 APRIL
11.00PM

Felt terrible this morning. Shower made no difference. Busy weekends are fun; but no fun. I'm sure you know what I mean? Work is currently no fun.

My wife's still trying to adjust to the new nursery hours. Which basically means our eldest is at home more, so my wife's more tired. It can't be easy. How she juggles everything is incredible. I can barely look after myself and hate myself, for it.

TUESDAY 11 APRIL
I DON'T CARE WHAT TIME IT IS

A nothing day - I felt nothing and could not contribute anything. A period I wasted and will never get back. I was just an empty shell.

WEDNESDAY 12 APRIL
11.00PM

Not working tomorrow – my wife needs my help. I'm sure my company is losing its patience, but I'm not unwell. And technically I'm taking my holiday. It's not a luxury. Don't remember the last time I had time off when either myself, or someone else, wasn't poorly.

My dad's not happy because I've fell out with my sister. All this has impacted on my mental health. I just wish everything was simple and that everyone was happy.

The mania is very much part of me; and wild.

Time to try and relax, our eldest will be up in six hours.

THURSDAY 13 APRIL
8.00PM

Luckily my wife isn't as bad as we thought. She's moving okay but being careful. I really dug in today. I did loads around the house and had some quality time with Bubba. Tomorrow we're doing lunch for her family. I'll just run around cleaning and looking after the girls like I normally do at family functions.

This afternoon I had some quality time with our eldest too. Huge tantrums about any little thing and screams and tears start from nowhere. It's a battle of wills. You're never left wondering how she feels. Me? I just felt like raking my eyes out every time my heart beats.

I'm beginning to regret my blow up on Sunday. I was right, but feel I've created more problems than I've solved. Now the guilt is flooding my heart and head.

I'm sitting here having a bit of a moment. But we all have them, don't we? You look at how many years you've been on the earth. How you've lived your life. Hopes and dreams - your successes; failures and fears. How you quantify your life. Well spent? Or wasted? Enough time to change? Accepting you've messed it all up? Or content with your lot? In the last two years, I've tried to undo some of the pain from the previous twenty; despite my mental health being poor. I think now, if my life ended naturally or I ended it - I'd be okay with my efforts. Ten years ago? I'd have died full of pain, angst and regret.

GOOD FRIDAY
9.10PM

Flat out all day; but managed to order my wife's flowers...

Our eldest nearly ran out in front of a car at the super-market. I gave her a rocket, then bunged her into her buggy

- no nonsense discipline. The guilt I'm feeling is shredding my insides. Sometimes I hate being a parent; and hate myself. Honestly? I just want to shut myself in a room and sob.

We're just about ready for the third annual Easter egg hunt.

My wife thinks Bubba has teeth coming down. I don't think my mind or body can take more unbroken sleep; crying, or pain.

On the way to the garden today we walked passed the church. Our eldest said *Daddy*, why do people go to church? I couldn't believe it. She's three; what sort of question is that?! I just said that some people go to church to celebrate what they believe in. I was never going to say what I really think…

I'm slightly less manic and have a little more control over my head. But I'm still struggling socially. For someone like me, who's always been very social and tactile, it's excruciating, debilitating and devastating. Sometimes I feel soulless. Then I go to the other extreme - bursting with emotion and tears.

Hopefully it'll be a nice day tomorrow. I want my ladies to enjoy their special days.

EASTER SATURDAY -
THE EASTER EGG HUNT AND MY BEAUTIFUL WIFE'S BIRTHDAY
10.00PM

The flowers were beautiful. And delivered bang on time. My wife loved them; especially as she wasn't expecting anything. It was chaos prior to the egg hunt. We had a manic hour trying to get ready, but it was worth it. Two hours of egg-fuelled mayhem followed. And so much chocolate! My favourite was the piñata.

I said to my wife I wanted an adult one. So, when you whack it alcoholic miniatures stream out - shades of my past; present; and future. Maybe I'll have one at my wake…That would be perfect.

We rounded off with a Chinese. The ladies were all exhausted; and went to bed early.

It's the happiest I've been in days. But the darkness lasted much longer this time. It's not currently affecting people around me. The day my eldest can tell I'm not right, is the day I'll need professional help, again.

EASTER SUNDAY
LATE

Today was calmer. Chilled - like the obscene amount of chocolate in the fridge.

I woke up feeling okay, no mania. My mind still scatty, but my body not feeling like it had to be moving continuously. That was a relief. I hate the squirming feeling - when it's impossible to get comfortable. Or hold a train of thought.

We went to a local stately home with Nanny and Grandad for another egg hunt. The grounds are lovely. Just what we needed after yesterday; what I needed. I'm so much more relaxed out in the open air. No real boundaries or structure.

Our eldest was pushed down a hill in her buggy and free-wheeled solo to the bottom. Not the safest thing I've seen. But she loved it. She's fearless, currently the polar-opposite of me.

I'm paranoid my own shadow hates me.

Next was a trip to a pub opposite my nan's house. And you've guessed it… Another egg-hunt! I was physically and emotionally spent so opted for a pint of lager and a chat and a cuddle with Nan.

I'm drunk. Rum; take a bow.

EASTER MONDAY
8.00PM

Yup - the hangover was nasty. Thumping, throbbing head; couldn't quench my thirst. Rum sweats. I kept falling asleep in the chair like I'm doing now. My eyes are heavy. Today was a struggle. It's my own fault. And I know it. Sometimes my behaviour makes no sense.

We went to a local farm this afternoon. It was a really nice change…. I still felt rancid.

It was a nice end to a long weekend, even though I'm now feeling physically and mentally drained. I was desperate to get the girls in bed, so I could rest. Now that's awful parenting. Just a touch selfish don't you think? I honestly didn't care though. I wish I did.

Work was hard. Barely spoke to anyone. A couple of people worry about it. Most don't care. It's easier that way. I don't want pity, just to be able to try and get on with my life.

The house is a mess. The girls are a handful. Our eldest is becoming stroppy. She hates being told 'no'. It's hard. She tells me I upset her. But what can you do? Not discipline your children? Let them run wild? And grow up not understanding right and wrong, and respect? 'Course you can't.

I'm tired now; of everything. Feels like I'm just going through the motions – time is passing me by, days I'll never get back. Many people live life like it is infinite. Not appreciating everything around them. I know I'm guilty. My nan seems to be stable. Very thin, but still getting out the house. That's the main thing. Staying active, feeling loved; having a purpose.

The family unit is getting stronger. But I still feel disconnected. It's irrational. I hate it. But it's me.

WEDNESDAY 19 APRIL
9.30PM

The tiredness won't relent. Work was hard - there's job uncertainty everywhere. I just hoped nobody would talk to me.

I had my annual appraisal this morning. Had a poor year therefore a poor appraisal. But I don't care about proving how good I am. I just wanted to get out of there. I'm my own worst critic, especially outside of work (my impossible standards). In work, I currently, honestly don't care what people think.

The grumpy house rumbles on. Our eldest has a strop every time she doesn't get what she wants. She's hysterical; loud, noisy and disruptive, with anger in her eyes. Directed at me; the man who shouts, who tells her off and makes her cry. It just reinforces my belief that I'm a failure. But hopefully one day it'll change.

THURSDAY 20 APRIL
8.00PM

Very manic - it was difficult to control. The slightest thing can change my mood. Pick me up. Bring me down. Irrationality, imbalance and paranoia - it's always there.

I spent the day avoiding conversations with work colleagues. It's quite easy. If you're on the phone, you can't talk to other people. But people were pulling me about it. I think I just smiled uncomfortably, making comments to look like I was okay. Or I just looked away. It's something I'm doing more of.

Parenting doesn't get easier. It's physically and emotionally demanding. It's worth it of course it is. Doesn't mean to say that it's always enjoyable... Amazing and beautiful highs but crushing; demoralising lows.

Our eldest's language is developing rapidly; as is her intellectual curiosity. She can pretty much dress herself now and doesn't like help. She's her own person. No doubt.

Bubba is eleven weeks today. Insane! She's growing into her features now and becoming a lady. Both are firecrackers; just like their mum. In a decade I'm going to be in trouble. Deep trouble...

Time for a beer... I've no idea why I wrote in the singular.

FRIDAY 21 APRIL
9.10PM

Last night my insomnia was bad. By the time I crashed our eldest woke.

Today, well at least the most part, was about my wife. (We'd planned to get our eldest some shoes.) She had a decent amount of birthday money and wanted to do some shopping. When we got there, I took the girls - giving her some proper shopping time. She was ages, exactly what I'd hoped – and when we met up had loads of gear and a smile on her face.

It's time for her to start taking some time back. I do it enough.

I bought a cup of tea for a guy sleeping rough. It wasn't a cold day, but he was very grateful. We both walked away happy. The cost...? Just a pound – and the outcome...? I'm not sure it's right to quantify human spirit.

It was a nice morning; precious family time. My head was floating, endorphins flowing. I was so happy. Not a care in the world. I honestly don't remember when I last felt like that.

I bailed on three social invites tonight. Everyone is getting hammered as I write. The up side is that nobody will be missing me or bothered that I'm not out. So, there's no guilt. But the fact I have so many invites is an indication of how bad my paranoia might be.

SATURDAY 22 APRIL
10.30PM

It was nice catching up with my dad... One too many beers though... My uncle didn't turn up. He's a lovely guy but has so much going on. It's not surprising he gets caught up in other things.

Looks like my sister is getting her own place - the move is Tuesday. I hope she settles and is truly happy.

Came back from the pub and guess what? My eldest wanted to go out, so we walked to the park near our house. It was lovely. Warm, and chilled. Then we went to the pub on the way home. They have a huge garden. We played footie and hide and seek. We both loved it.

Got a text about half eleven from a mate telling me to make myself available for drinks tomorrow. It felt like the invitation was an after-thought. I made my feelings clear, that I wasn't happy. Not like me.

Woke up hanging...

Dry mouth and a throbbing head. Stomach cramps; awful.

I looked after the girls while my wife went to a boot fair. About ten minutes after she left I burst into tears - sobbing uncontrollably, tears streaming down my face. I was cuddling Bubba. Luckily our eldest was in her room. I'd never want her to see me like that.

It came out the blue. I won't tell my wife. I imagine the first time she'll find out is when she reads this. I've no idea how she'll react. Hopefully she'll understand - even if she isn't happy. My mental health hasn't been great. I'm finding it hard talking to people. The main problem is I listen to other people and sometimes think *My God that's boring.* Then I think. *Do I bore people to tears? Do people want to listen? Is anyone interested?* So most of the time I just don't bother saying anything. Sounds insane doesn't it? I'm totally bent out of shape.

I left my WhatsApp group too. It's not attention seeking - quite the opposite. I don't want attention, or to be fussed over. I just need to focus on the day to day stuff - just my house, my family, work and my mental health.

Our eldest luckily had an okay night. I still worry about her though. It's the night terrors. And she's always telling people to go away. And that they're upsetting her. She says that about me every day. I'm paranoid she'll end up hating me - makes you question your whole being. Or maybe it's just me? This perfectly illustrates my challenges. And those faced by so many of us. It's not just about being a nutter. That's how I describe myself to friends. Puts people at ease. Makes us smile. Sometimes humour is the best therapy.

I have no idea what people will make of this. What you're making of this? Whether you've never suffered from this illness… Or are suffering and taking each day as it comes; or suffering in silence - or living with someone who is. Whatever, I truly hope you're taking something from this.

I'm sure my wife will say there have been periods when living with me has been profoundly difficult; painful and frustrating. But in time we do open-up. Some people get there more quickly than others. It's just about feeling ready; which is a deeply individual thing. I don't want men to feel afraid to talk about their feelings anymore. The more we talk; the better husbands, dads, brothers, sons and friends we'll be... And the happier we'll be. And the more lives we'll save.

Nutter... (It just makes me laugh). I'd never say that at work. People would either be offended or embarrassed. The workplace, and the world, has gone PC mad. It's ridiculous. You can't say anything about anything. I hate it.

Bubba's now grabbing toys. And sitting up! She's so strong, so developed. It's crazy. She's growing so fast and she was big from the off! I came home through the door and our eldest grabbed my hand; walked me to the kitchen and showed me the cornflake cakes she'd made. Then we ate them together - magic.

At bedtime she told me she wanted to learn how to read. I was so proud. I love how clever she is. Started to think about what I'll say to her if this is ever published. My aim is to help change lives, to encourage people to think *it is* okay *not* to be okay - to be sad, lonely, depressed and vulnerable. To feel lost, angry, paranoid and afraid. And that it's okay to talk about your problems and feelings, to admit you need help, and accept help.

TUESDAY 25 APRIL
TEETHING

It's begun... The dribbling; raised temperatures. The restlessness and winging... And I don't mean just me...

Less than three months into her life. It has started. You know? When you rub your little finger along the gums and it feels like sandpaper? They're pushing down. And will start breaking through soon. Her cheeks are so tender and round. She's clingy and very cuddly – and looks deep into your eyes when she hugs you. And smiles when she knows we're there. It's amazing to be that person.

Our eldest is being so comforting and kind. My wife has done an amazing job...

I'm feeling better, the best this week. The house is functioning well.

But she's just started crashing around in her bed. The smile might be gone soon...

WEDNESDAY 26 APRIL
NIGHT TERRORS AND BAD DREAMS

She woke at three o'clock crying. Then every ten minutes until four-fifty. It was both heartbreaking and exasperating. I'm sure she felt I was losing my temper. How could she not? Surely this would test anyone? Or it is just me being selfish again? I hate being so uncertain of myself.

I think it's just the years of bullying, piss taking and self-deprecation. It's why I can't take compliments. But I'll make sure the girls are never made to feel like this.

Looking back, spending so much of my time drunk and stoned didn't help me. I thought I was having fun, being one of the lads. I thought smoking would make everything go away. I was wrong. If I'd properly understood my mental illness, then - I would've never touched the stuff.

Pot (filled) holes

Back in my teens, always so cocky,
Always the lad, walked with a swagger
The truth is my teens were somewhat rocky,
Boy, did I drink my weight in lager

But one day after a terrible tiff,
The lager was just no longer enough
I decided to puff on a weedy spliff,
The first few puffs I felt fucking rough

The deeper the drags, the bigger the haze
My problems began to drift away,
I began to smile, in a smoke-filed daze,
Slept well at the end of my first smoking day

Smoked more and more as time went on
A way to help eradicate most of my pain,
Blowbacks from chillums, blunts and bongs
To escape, I passed out again and again.

I abused, not used, the drug for years
It became a close, non-judgemental friend
But it still didn't stop the pain and tears.
It did more harm than good in the end.

In fact, it made things so much worse

At least our eldest was happy when she woke up.

I'm now experiencing both insomnia and bad dreams. It takes me hours to drift off. Then if I do, fifteen minutes later I wake up. Wide eyed, buzzing, messed-up head. I think it's because I've felt manic recently. So even when I lay down my mind is still rushing and bursting.

THURSDAY 27 APRIL
10.00PM

Work was slightly more comfortable today. I found talking to people a little easier, but then I started to worry. Am I working hard enough? Are my stats suffering? Uncontrollable guilt whatever the situation…

The day went quickly. Apart from the fact I left my bag in the garden after my lunch. A mind blank - shows how wired I am. Totally distracted and detached. Too much on my mind for it to cope. It's why I lost my wallet two weeks ago.

The girls were ratty when I got home; and brought me down. Not their fault and I'll make sure they know that. It's because my emotions are so finely balanced. I struggle to control things. I'm on a tight-rope - and wobbling.

It's still lovely to spend time with them.

FRIDAY 28 APRIL
11.38PM

Bad dreams and teething kept my girls up most of the night so no real lay-in for us. But you don't expect it as parents, do you?

Our eldest couldn't wait for us to leave my parents' house. She wanted Nanny and Grandad to herself. So, a peaceful afternoon then? No chance! I cleaned the fridges and car. Fixed the sofa wheels and did a huge shop. Stripped all the beds; and by the time I sat down I was knackered. Not as tired as my wife though. She had a very bad night and needs rest. No, I'm not tired. My mind is winding down. But the rushes and mania are nasty.

It's weird not having our eldest here. The house feels empty. The sooner I can get to sleep, the sooner she'll be home.

Rushes

Twitching fingers, scratching skin
Uncontrollable head, I can feel it begin

Mentally rushing, my mind is flooding
So many thoughts, my heart is pounding

As the pace quickens and I lose control
And disconnect from the outside world

I'm totally consumed, the mania's rampaging
In half an hour, it's years I'm ageing

Narrowing eyes, heads in my hands
My internal struggle, there's no magic wand

The impossible speed begins to slow
Tension easing from head to toe

But as my eyes widen and the control comes back
It won't be long until the mania's back

And the rushes

SATURDAY 29 APRIL
A STAR IS BORN

Flat out until our eldest got home. She was proper ratty; I just had to let her work it out herself. While providing guidance and discipline as required. It's not easy.

In the end we went out - first on the scooter, then to visit Nanny and play football. I love that she kicks with both feet. The fact she's so free - my polar-opposite.

It was the big fight - Joshua vs Klitschko. I didn't feel up to going to a house party, so I watched it on my own in the living room. It's times like this I really miss my grandad. He loved boxing; all the proper heavyweights – Clay (who became Ali), Liston, Cooper, Frazier and the rest - beautiful boxers in atmospheric black and white. It was undoubtedly the sports' golden era.

People say time heals all wounds. I think it just makes things more manageable. Open would heal. Scars last forever.

Our eldest is seriously whiny. Not sure if it's a jealousy thing. She's always been so independent. Now she's clingy and whingey. And it's a battle to get her to do anything herself. I refuse to back down, but I'm paying a heavy price. Your daughter repeatedly telling you she doesn't like you is one of the lowest and saddest places you'll ever be.

I woke up with a sore head. I wasn't immobile; just sluggish. But that's what happens when you drink. You know what the end game is - how you'll feel. But we still do it don't we? We don't go out to the pub just to see friends... You could go to a coffee shop! No, it's to drink alcohol.

Again, it's about whether you admit it to yourself or not. That sounds depressing. But I think it is very balanced. You've got to see things for what they are surely? I'm comfortable with the choices I make and how I manage myself. So long as you're in control you've got half a chance. If you start to lose control, that's when things, and you, deteriorate. I've seen what addiction can do to people... And you're seeing and reading about what it's done to me.

Had a shave; the first in a week. Had to look in the mirror... I didn't like it. I can see myself getting fatter. I wobble.

Imagine a bluebell walk... Sties, narrow gates, rocky fields and bursts of heavy rain... Plus a pram and buggy! It was laugh-out loud stuff. Us standing in a field getting lashed on! While the girls were snug under their waterproof covers. They laughed so much they gave themselves hiccups!

Nan came over with Dad in the afternoon. She looked thin, but content; and even fed and cuddled Bubba. It was wonderful.

I look and feel fat. It's constantly on my mind, I'm a barrel.

SIX. PARANOIA, GAMBLING AND BAD PARENTING

MONDAY 1 MAY
11.05PM

We had a training course today run by an excellent external consultant. The last section was about mental health and lit my fire. Afterwards, instead of going back to work, we had a long chat - about his work and my plans. We've shared some of the same challenges in life, so got on well from the start. If this ever takes off, it would be great to work with him in the future. He's a good guy.

TUESDAY 2 MAY
8.15PM

The girls are poorly, but such brave girls. My wife's brilliant. Powering on; keeping things ticking over. She's the love of my life and our rock.

Fell out with Dad over family stuff. I say how I feel now and am honest. I'm past caring if people don't like it.

The girls have settled. I'm writing on a stopwatch. Looking at the clock; checking my phone for the message telling me to get my arse upstairs to help. Borrowed time... Not quiet time.

I'll be back at work in eleven hours. What a depressing thought. I'm a slave to the rat-race; while my life ebbs away. But that's the case for most of us, right?

Enough... My mind's starting to rush. I'm putting a lid on it. Otherwise, I'll be watching the sun rise.

WEDNESDAY 3 MAY
8.55PM

I spoke to quite a few people at work today. It was nice; felt good. But then I felt guilty because I wasn't working. And people regularly comment about others pulling their weight; or not. I hate being like this. Some people call it conscientious; I call it irrational and paranoid.

Bubba had a jab today. The nurse said she was amazing. She was grotty this evening. Or course she'd be! Three months old and had a massive needle shoved in her leg! Tonight, Calpol and cuddles are the remedy.

Our eldest was so lovely, gave so many cuddles. No surprise Bubba loves her so much. You can see it in her eyes... It melts my heart.

Me? I'm ticking along. The mania seems to have settled down a bit. I'm sleeping a little better. Well the last two nights at least. I don't have as much family baggage - ditched it. And I won't be taking it on again either. It's pointless. Here's the thing. You take things on and what happens? People resent you. Nobody listens; everyone gets defensive. Do you get any thanks? Like hell you do. How do you feel afterwards? Like, why did I bother? That's how.

THURSDAY 4 MAY
6.00PM

Woke up tired - too much sleep! Bubba is settling after her jab. But her teeth are still causing a problem. Calpol... A parent's best friend!

Apart from that though. My god - what a beautiful miracle she is. Three months tomorrow. It's sad thinking I'll never experience having a new baby again. I can understand why some people have large families.

FRIDAY 5 MAY
11.55PM

My wife is managing so well. She's a far better role model than I'll ever be. The mania means I'm so up and down. When I'm on form I'm 'Super Dad'. But when I'm not right? The fuse is short - I need to deal with my issues better.

Our eldest...? Well the battery that never goes flat. She's got rhythm. She's so clever and indescribably beautiful. She's tall with huge eyes and long straight hair. I pity the lads who come to the house when she gets older - her first boyfriends are in for a rough ride. I make no excuses. I'll be the same with both. Sorry girls. Only because I love you so much x

I hate this time of night. I can feel myself going through the tiredness. I'll be up for hours. It's soul-destroying and inevitable.

I'd be lost without Netflix.

SATURDAY 6 MAY
10.07AM

We drove to collect a double buggy. We (my wife) bought it on eBay for ninety-nine pence! You're right. What a joke. I thought it was going to be a piece of junk. But we didn't find out. They weren't in - brilliant. I just stood on their drive chuckling. What else can you do? The little tests – I feel like I'm being provoked every day. And must try hard not to take the bait - to snap, to lose it. Can't remember how many times a smile has been the cover for boiling blood.

Then it was off to our eldest's friends' birthday party. She had fun, but was very mischievous – had the devil in her... I spent ages in the little ball-pit with Bubba and did some selfies. It was lovely. It also meant my wife got to sit down and spend time with her friends. And relax a little bit. Oh, and I didn't have to speak to people.

SUNDAY 7 MAY
7.30PM

Boot fair...

It was rubbish. Weather was rank too. I fell out with our eldest because she refused to keep her coat on. I walked away; came back and she was cold and crying. It drove me nuts - *the guilt. The guilt.... Sometimes it makes me so hot my skin tingles. What on earth must parents around me have thought?*

At bedtime we all went to our eldest's room. She was using my back as a slide. But one time planted both feet on my calf. I went ballistic. I lost it. She ran out the room crying. My wife cried too. I felt ashamed - utterly ashamed. One of those moments in your life you'd give anything to take back. But wear like a stain on your soul for the rest of your days.

I've been stretched on the sofa for ages... Just replaying it in my head; trying to rationalise my guilt. The self-loathing makes me want to cut myself. I'm deeply raking my arms with my finger-nails. I wear short sleeve shirts at work. So really need to stop. Otherwise they'll look terrible tomorrow. They're bad already.

MONDAY 8 MAY
9.50PM

I still feel sick thinking about last night.

Work was hard. It's the first time in a while I've been properly concerned about my mental state. I'm hyper-emotional and seriously imbalanced. Don't get me wrong; I don't want to be a robot. But I need to be more stable than I am now.

I'm taking tomorrow off - got to sort out some new (herbal) meds. They worked before. Hopefully they will again.

My eldest's stutter is the worst it's been for ages. It's totally my fault. She's so beautiful, so full of love. She doesn't deserve to be shouted at the way I did. I feel awful; I can't hold back the tears. I need some time to process what I've done and how I feel. Every time I'm on my own I start to cry. But it's what I deserve.

TUESDAY 9 MAY
MEDICATION

I've held off long enough. I can't any more. I need something to help me. I'm fighting but not winning. This time I'll look at something stronger. It's the mania, paranoia and insomnia. I need to regain some emotional balance and get some quality sleep.

I take Valerian-Hops which come from an Asian plant. It tastes like horrible. Main side effect is diarrhoea.

The tablets are called 5-HTP. 5-HTP works in the brain and central nervous system by increasing the production of the chemical serotonin. Serotonin can affect sleep, appetite, temperature, sexual behavior, and pain sensation. Serotonin is believed to play an important role in depression, insomnia, obesity, and many other conditions.

The main side effects are diarrhoea, again - but also crazy dreams. I'm already having these. The pills seem like a big step. I need time to think. If in two weeks I'm not improving. I'll have to re-assess. I might book a therapy session or get a medication consultation. I'd prefer the former.

Serotonin

Sunrise Serotonin struggles
Every sinew frantically juggles,
Rapidly increasing volume of thought
Outwardly calm, internally taught,
Trying for balance to get through the day,
Often unsure of what I should say
Now the end of the day and everyone's in bed
I'm left alone with the thoughts in my head
Night time Serotonin struggles

Repeat

Now this is important. There's no shame in going through what I am. And you must understand that. There's no shame in talking to professionals. I've used homeopaths, therapists, and doctors. And I'll use them again, whenever I think I need them. If you're worried, only tell people you really trust. I just blew everything open - told everyone. Bottling pain and trauma up made me so unwell. I've told you about the three times I've contemplated and the once I've attempted suicide. I wouldn't want you; or anyone dear to you, to have to go through that. Honestly, trust me. Getting help and showing the true you are the only way to go. And if people love you they'll support you. If you need help; I'm begging you, please, please take that step. Talking changes lives...

WEDNESDAY 10 MAY
9.50PM

Felt very low and dark this morning. Head fried; worried about work. My herbal drops taste like failure.

Spoke to my head of department today. Mainly the paranoia and the fact I'm generally struggling. I'll always try to be honest with people. It's the right thing to do. No matter how painful.

Our eldest's stuttering is no better. It's breaking my heart. We got an NHS appointment through today, so we'll see what happens. I still blame myself. I love her so much.

THURSDAY 11 MAY
LATE

One of my worst days as a parent. I felt like breaking down; like giving up. I feel so low. My insomnia is stronger than the drops.

I'm trying so hard to not agitate my eldest. To really make her feel relaxed…

So, what happened?

I took her to bed. She had a meltdown in the bathroom - just because I wouldn't carry her to bed. So, she shut herself in the nursery. Then had a strop in bed because I couldn't find a book she wanted. My wife came in. Found the book. Read her a story and calmed her down. I felt and must've looked like a monster. I felt sick in my stomach. I couldn't eat. Still can't. I've told my wife I'm backing right off. I'm not forcing my eldest to do anything with me anymore. I've even stopped asking for cuddles. Why? I figure if she wants to she'll come to me.

No chance of sleeping anytime soon. It's the paranoia and self-loathing. I'm scared this will never end. That she'll stop loving me. From my brain pulsing to the tips of my toes, mania is uncontrollable.

FRIDAY 12 MAY
9.58PM

A breakthrough with our eldest; I'm so relieved. We all went to the ball-park. At first, she still wasn't interested in me. I put my socks on to go play. She looked at me and said *Daddy, I don't like you - I don't want to play, go away.*

I sat down; heartbroken. But hiding it with a smile.

Later she had a fall and called for help so I ran up. This time I got a huge cuddle as we sat just chilling out. Then she asked me to play with her. And we ran around like we used to - it was brilliant. I was so happy. My wife more relieved I think.

My mental health isn't brilliant; but slowly improving. My wife can see it. And it's making me less on edge. My eldest must know when I'm not right. Surely you if you're a parent you know this too?

Her stutter seems to be easing. No coincidence is it?

SATURDAY 13 MAY
11.40PM

Fair to say I've had a few. Our eldest is sleeping terribly. So restless and has a sore throat - super grouchy.

Day started well - and ended not so well. I met a close friend and had a quick catch up. It's the classic car festival in town, so food and beer stalls all around the town centre. Then met Dad; our eldest got her face painted… Happy days…

Things are manic. Nan's unwell again.

How would you feel about taking medication that changes your moods and emotions? Would you find it easy to make the decision to take them? I found it very hard. But if you're in this position and experiencing these things; remember. It's the right decision - therapy, pharmaceutical drugs, homeopathic medicine. Use what you need. What you can cope with. And what will help make you feel better. The only person who truly knows is you. Fuck me; and fuck everyone else too. You're the only one who matters.

Now the beer starts. And the writing stops.

SUNDAY 14 MAY
8.30PM

Tired and hungover, as expected. I messaged Mum - I had to meet her and explain why I'd recently fell out with Dad, and what was going on.

It wasn't about sides or justifying my actions. Or sympathy - we're all adults. I wanted to explain what was happening. You'd think it would make it feel better? It made me very sad. I even said that to Mum.

The rest of the afternoon was good. We were all tired, the ladies poorly too. But the simple family time is so enjoyable. And I'm feeling so much better now I'm starting to get closer to my eldest again. My guilt and self-loathing are easing. But they're still there... My second shadow...

MONDAY 15 MAY
11.50PM

I've still not visited Nan. The guilt is returning; the shadow darkening. I know what to do to stop it. So why don't I just do it? These are internal struggles we all experience; me many times every day. Maybe I just don't want to see Nan so poorly? After holding my auntie's hand, the day before she passed I'm not sure I'm ready to go through all that again so soon - self, self; self.

My wife has aggravated her shoulder and back. And my eldest hasn't slept well all week.

Haven't shaved for over a week - I'm a ragged mess.

TUESDAY 16 MAY
10.00PM

The house had a terrible night; again. Bubba was up regularly. Our eldest had a meltdown around midnight and didn't reset-tle until about two in the morning. Night after night, this'll push anyone to the brink of their capabilities, resilience and sanity. I'm already too close to insanity for comfort. If this goes on for much longer, I'll be down to one ear...

My wife woke up tired and grumpy; can't blame her... I wish I could just go back to sleep quickly. This is my biggest current problem. But if you're having these issues, controlled legal drugs might really help. You might be thinking, *Well, he's writing a lot about having a drink at weekends. Alcohol is both dangerous and addictive.* You're right. But I had my destruc-tive drinking phase when I was younger - when my girlfriend dumped me after returning from travelling. I was in a dark place then, very low, deeply depressed and alone. It took me a long time to pull myself out of that. It was also then when

I was at the depths of my gambling, and went to GA. I never told anyone about that either. I had a lot going on. Anyway, I'm comfortable managing alcohol. But I'd never touch a fruit machine again - ever.

My (old) five a day

When I was at college, I loved my fruit
But it wasn't your healthy conventional route,

The ones I liked they didn't have peel
They were printed on a fruit machine reel,

For five a day it could cost just a pound
Now for a student that's financially sound,

But soon my addiction was brutal and bold
Gambling nudges; what should I hold?

Spending so much and getting so pissed
Ignoring my mates, they weren't people I missed,

I hit rock bottom, flat broke and alone
Last chance was attending G.A. in Maidstone

Stories of lies; self-harm and shame
But together we bonded and healed our pain

It took me a while, admittance the worst
But it beat the alternative; my taxi, a hearse

My wife picked me up. Both girls crashed out in the back. Worst case scenario. Its past ten o'clock and they're unsettled. We need a better night - I need a better night.

Properly upset stomach. I'm tired, stressed; haven't eaten for ages. Now the headaches are starting again.

Still haven't had a shave.

WEDNESDAY 17 MAY
8.45PM

Up most of the night; shakes and evil sweats - couldn't get comfortable. Hot then cold, hot then cold. My head was soaked at one point. The toilet seat was still warm in the morning because I spent so much time on it.

Work wasn't as bad; even though I felt mentally and physically unwell. I didn't even let anyone make me a drink and I didn't eat. That way I didn't need to visit the toilet.

Dad picked me up; on his own. I was thinking 'here we go, here comes another lecture'. Luckily it didn't materialise.

The house has fallen silent. I need my beauty sleep - no idea how many days it's been since I last looked in a mirror.

THURSDAY 18 MAY
9.05PM

Probably my best day at work since Christmas. It shows hard work does pay off. But I still didn't feel proud, or any sense of achievement (although I feigned it a bit just to look what society views as normal). It just meant the day was easier.

My wife picked me up. Both girls were asleep again, so we decided to pick up chips on way home - big mistake. Girls were screaming when I got back to the car and barely stopped all the way home. My wife lost it and I don't for one second blame her. I never blame her for anything. Not after everything she's put up with from me.

Not sure if I'll have to upgrade to tablets now. That would be massive. I'm not getting carried away. The way I've been over the last few weeks I could lapse at any time.

Things with our eldest are much better. I hope my wife can see I'm trying to make things right.

FRIDAY 19 MAY
10.30PM

Lost my patience with the house, it was a total mess. My wife took the girls to soft play. I cleaned top to bottom; then re-arranged the kitchen. I was knackered and irritable by the time they came home.

Our eldest still needed burning out so we went to see my nan... I'm so pleased we did. I thought she looked poorly. She said her Chemotherapy isn't working – but blood transfusions are. How long will they do these for? Who knows?

We took some beautiful photos. I'm so happy with them. And I was even in one - kept my promise to my dad too.

Today was washing. Well this morning anyway. There were clothes on every floor of the house. Felt like gouging my eyes out. My skin was crawling. Luckily our eldest was good, so got loads done. It feels good to do more. I feel tired but more at peace – less guilt; and a bit more comfortable in my own skin.

Our eldest stacked it twice at the nature park; she is so much like me. My wife is always saying it. But she is; although she's more beautiful. And already has a better memory. Hopefully she'll be a far superior version of me - a less complicated version of me; a happier version of me. I'll be doing everything I can to make sure that happens.

12.30AM

I've just woken up face down on the floor; food all around me. What a state and a disgrace. Our girls are having a terrible night.

SUNDAY 21 MAY

8.30PM

I woke up with loads of energy - no Sunday hangover. My wife was feeling pants. So at least I was the other end of the spectrum. We had breakfast at the boot fair. Five times our eldest spilled her drink in a couple of minutes! After that it was the farm-train, which is becoming a regular thing. It's nice for my wife to have quality time with our children.

In the afternoon I took Bubba for a walk around the lake. It was serene. I'm not sure how long it's been since I used that word. I also had a shave. First time I've looked in the mirror for about a month. I felt like I was getting a little bit of my swagger back.

I'm still taking my meds and have no intention of stopping. I need to keep looking after myself. (I'll keep saying this. You need to look after yourself. I don't care if I sound like a scratched record. Know yourself. Sounds like a load of hippie crap, right? Wrong. Understanding yourself will help you to start identifying and solving your problems. Trust me on this one - got the scars and memories to prove it.) I'm happy. I hope it continues.

MONDAY 22 MAY
8.20PM

I came home to a house of full on carnage. And some comedian parked in our space in front of our living room window. The girls were absolutely wired. From the minute I stepped in I did not stand still for two hours. A fifteen-hour day and counting...

I'm feeling more stable and stronger. I'm finding difficult and stressful situations a little easier to deal with. I only say it under hushed tones. But I seem to be on an upward curve.

I'm sure my wife can sense and feel it. That's currently the trouble though - the mania. My highs and lows are blatant and extreme. It seems to be more part of my life than the paranoia, which is marginally better I suppose...

Coping mechanisms are so important. My main ones these days are fishing and walking. It used to be booze and blackouts - occasionally it still is.

TUESDAY 23 MAY
11.50PM

Last night? A young man, just twenty-three years of age, detonated a suicide bomb as teenagers left an Ariana Grande gig. The current death toll is twenty-two. It's so sad...

We were late for our speech therapy assessment. The therapist confirmed our eldest has a moderate stutter; but excellent language skills. We were given some techniques to try. But the therapist also said we were doing a great job raising her. I never think I am. I credit everything good about the girls to my wife. They have no allocated space until October so if it gets worse, we'll go private.

Bubba's eczema has really flared up; all over her body. I just want to cuddle her. But I have so much body heat. I can't for long.... It makes me so sad, makes me want to cry. She's not sad though - taking everything in her stride.

I'm feeling good; the third day on the bounce. Work has been okay. I'm not dreading my shifts. Feels like I'm talking a bit more too. It's a nice, but unusual feeling.

Dad said Nan's blood is the best it's been for months which is a lovely surprise.

My wife is less tired. Because I'm feeling better I'm doing more around the house.

I need to go take my meds; I forgot this morning...

Better Days

It might sound like my life is frequently bad
A mad, sad, dysfunctional dad,
But there are also so many lovely days too
Happy thoughts, making memories, not feeling blue,

Which means I can be the real me
The man I want everyone around me to see,
There's no better feeling than meaning a smile,
Relaxing, not stressing, just enjoying life, while

Being sensible and looking after my health,
Something more valuable than material wealth,
On Good days I feel warm, and life just has flow
Looking in the mirror, a welcome glow,

To my face, and it's something I'd like to keep,
On good days I even enjoy my sleep

THURSDAY 25 MAY
5.30PM

Comedy and nightmare moment this morning – as I got out of the shower, I heard our eldest at the bottom of the stairs calling me. I asked her to wait a minute. Then the doorbell started ringing continuously.

What was going on? Turns out my wife went out front to water the flowers. Then our eldest shut the door behind my wife and locked it! It was seriously naughty. But secretly I was very impressed. When I asked her why she did it her response was *I don't know daddy.* Then she burst into tears. I couldn't bring myself to tell her off. Yeah. I know it's weak. It was my choice.

After I comforted my wife things were okay. She was just petrified at the thought of this happening when I wasn't there. I totally get it.

Mentally I'm feeling more able to take things in my stride. I might even start using mirrors again. I just need to be prepared to look in to them properly. And be comfortable with what I see, whatever that is…

FRIDAY 26 MAY
SUNSET

We had a lovely breakfast. Our eldest was so happy and behaved beautifully. But my breakfast included chips and black pudding… I didn't read the menu. Fat bastard, you're probably saying, (or maybe that's just my paranoia...) I left stuffed and embarrassed. Looking at the floor.

Our eldest then went off to spend the night at Nanny and Grandad's. We went back and did some housework.

Took my meds and then came here; the lake. It's glorious. I've missed it. Not so much the fishing, but the quiet time, the peace. All I can hear is birdsong and a large frog jumping around by my feet.

SATURDAY 27 MAY
8.30PM

I'm shattered, can't even be bothered to eat. I'm barely able to write. I had to pack up in a monsoon. It serves me right for going fishing; selfish twat.

Our eldest came back totally hyperactive. In the afternoon we went to my mate's gaff. We sank a few beers. Of course! The sun on my face, mates around me. I felt at ease; I was having fun.

She played with the big girls until she blew a gasket around half five. I took home in a taxi - her first time in a car with no booster seat... Landmark moment!

10.30PM

Woke up on the floor; fully clothed. Tongue stuck to the carpet. I peeled myself off the floor and dragged myself onto the sofa, still fully clothed.

Rum drunk - I love the taste. Love the warm feeling. Love everything about it. Not sure I'm even escaping. I enjoy drinking. I'm not ashamed. I'm a good person. I have a vice. Who doesn't?

On the way to the beach we stopped at a huge boot fair. No fun though – our eldest went ballistic. She burned herself out.

The beach was manic. She went on one ride and after a minute jumped off – repeatedly… Apparently money grows on trees! I'm a walking, talking cash machine. I thought it would be years until this started…

Around midnight a huge storm rolled in. Then the thunder and lightning started. It was deafening, and spectacular. It woke her up - obviously! But far from being scared, she was fascinated. We watched from the window. Flash after flash, bang after bang, both transfixed.

It was always going to be a bad night; it was her first storm. How could I expect her to kip after that! I just wrote it off.

MONDAY 29 MAY

8.00PM

One of her worst nights for ages… No idea what's wrong. I got about an hour and a half of shut eye. I look a mess. Need a shave. Need a haircut. Need to sleep.

Need a rest.

My wife was feeling bad, so I volunteered to take the girls for a walk in the double buggy. Then our eldest decided she wanted to go to town. At least they behaved. I was sweating sugar cane solution.

Our eldest was in bed early so another broken night beckons. But something lovely happened. I took Bubba for a walk and when I came back dinner was ready, the house quiet. My wife and I actually ate together. For about half an hour we just chilled and had a bit of a giggle. Honestly; I was so happy - it was wonderful. And I've missed that so much.

TUESDAY 30 MAY
EARLY HOURS

Got home and the girls were already in bed. We've got to break this cycle. And my bad eating - I feel fat and disgusting. I hate it. I hate my stomach. I LOOK LIKE SOMEONE STUFFED A BEER KEG UP MY JUMPER.

Our eldest has already been up for two hours. I'm in her room every fifteen minutes. No sign of it ending soon. It's not her fault. I just need to make her feel loved. Here we go again... This is really testing me, I often feel like I'm going to snap. Ever been so strung out you feel like putting your fist through a wall, door or window? Well I'm on that edge...

I didn't think the nights could get worse.

I was wrong; very wrong.

I think our eldest was up a dozen times. This morning she woke me up. Saw I was tired and said *Daddy. You look tired. Lay there. I'll read you stories.* I felt like crying. Everything melted away... She's incredible...I stepped out the door looking shambolic but glowing inside.

Bubba had her jabs today; and was grouchy when I got home. She's massive and so strong. Our eldest barely saw me but she still blew me away. We read a story and she spelled out the titles of her Mister Men books. I was so proud and gave her the hugest bear hug.

Seeing what's not there

A group of two or a heaving crowd,
The voices inside are always as loud
As tones become hushed, or people turn around,
My mind suffocated by familiar clouds

What had I said? What had I done?
Totally frozen but wanting to run
My heart beating fast, sweat on my face,
I'd kill to be anywhere, a different place

As I close my eyes and the mania recedes,
My head still pounding again I concede
The people didn't even know I was there,
Even less about me did they even care

What did they think? How must I appear?
My actions, their impressions, amongst my fears
As I walk away my head still bursting,
I'm angry, sad, tormented and cursing

The alternative world I live every day,
That affects every interaction in every way
But the hardest thing to accept by far,
Is its part of my being, I hate paranoia

SEVEN. SLEEPLESS NIGHTS AND MANIA

THURSDAY 1 JUNE
9.00PM

I was buzzing at work even though I've slept no more than twelve hours this week - my biggest problem is currently impatience. I have a short fuse and can't stand people wasting my time. Triggers are tiny and unpredictable.

The girls are struggling. The house is tetchy. The atmosphere sometimes crackles; sometimes pops. You can feel the electricity. Sometimes it's negative, but most of the time it's positive. At the moment I'm neither.

FRIDAY 2 JUNE
10.30PM

We've all done it haven't we? Started a job - mainly because the missus has been banging on about it and you've been meaning to do it for ages. Then a few minutes in thought 'Why did I bother?' That was me today. The garden was a jungle; it took ages to clear and tidy. Then there was the shed. Four hours later

179

I was done. It looked good, but I'd gone past caring. I was sick of the sight of it; and big watery blisters.

One thing that had come out the shed was our eldest's bike. And she wouldn't take her hands off it! So, the decision was made; this was her first attempt at riding a bike. A real rite of passage; I was so proud. I hope happy memories are flooding back for you. I still had a lump in my throat when we got home. My cheeks damp with tears. And they are now too.

SATURDAY 3 JUNE
21.22PM

The broken and stressful nights just keep coming. Finally got down about half one this morning. At twenty to four three ladies stumbled down the stairs.

I've now been up for seventeen hours...

The last two weeks have been hard. But we're coming through the other side together - and it feels good. We have our ups and downs. The occasional disagreement, but tell me a couple who doesn't?

This afternoon we went to a family fun day at a local pub. They had a huge garden full of arts and craft stalls, raffles etc. - as well as a magician; band and barbeque. It was a lovely. And our eldest is behaving so much better when we're out. All those times when I hated myself for being so strict are paying off a little bit.

The last hour before the girls went to bed I was short; snappy. There was no need for it. Our eldest was tired and Bubba has been teething. She's been so uncomfortable - so much dribbling, squawking, grumbling and chewing. She's normally such a happy little lady. I should be dishing out hugs and kisses – not attitude.

I'm not proud of myself; of course not. But I want to show *it is* okay not to be perfect. And that nobody has been, is, or ever will be. You've already seen I'm not. But you can also see I'm doing everything I can to be the best person I can. Nobody can ask any more of you than that.

SUNDAY 4 JUNE
9.45PM

Out little Bubba is so grumpy. When she's finding it hard; we're exhausted. And when she's asleep, we can't get to sleep. This might well bring back bad memories. Or maybe you're going though it right now. Empathy all round.

Our eldest has been so good all things considered. She's trying her best to help look after her little sister. She can also spell her own name now. Want a gauge to how quickly you're ageing? Watch how fast children grow; it's frightening. By the time I finish this; my girls will be four and one. And I'll be fifteen months off forty.

Feeling like I need some proper time off. It's not long - twelve working days. But when you're in this state of mind it feels like an eternity. Time can feel like it's going backwards and taking you with it.

A rough morning... My head was bad. Not manic - but dark and heavy. Walking into work I saw a beer bottle on a wall. I stopped. Crossed the road and picked it up. For a few seconds I thought... Should I break it and jam it into my neck? What would the pain be like? How long would it last? Would anyone care if I did it? Would it solve all my problems, and make everyone else's life easier? I honestly don't know why I have these thoughts. But I don't hide them anymore... Why should we? The answer is we shouldn't; ever... If you are, talk to someone; anyone. Please x

Arrived at work feeling rough - it was like I was living my life in slow motion - weirdly disconnected from people and the reality around me.

I'm feeling very introspective. I apologised to my wife for treating her so badly last summer. I don't even think I apologised then; horrible bastard.

She offered to do both monitors overnight for a few days. I said no. Point blank. Firstly, we need to feel like we contribute, don't we? Also, I've really been trying hard to be a better dad. Not raising my voice as much and using the counting to five techniques... And it seems to be working. Our eldest has started calling me *Beautiful Daddy*. It's one of the nicest things I'll ever hear. Something I'll take to my grave. Maybe she'll call me that at my funeral. That would be nice.

Our little Bubba is majorly into baby porridge. It's the way forward - to help her sleep longer. She's so big milk's already more of a drink than a meal. My dear, dear friend and his lovely lady are in Portugal. I sent a picture recently. He said our little Bubba looks exactly like my wife. For a man who spends most of his time swigging *Vinho Tinto Alentejano* to say they look alike they must do! They're both utterly beautiful, so he's pretty much spot on. He scrubs up okay. But he's punching well above his weight with his missus (it must be sympathy) - only busting your chops mate x

Our eldest was asleep on the floor when I got home. I carried her straight upstairs, put her night knickers on; hug then juice. She immediately went off. And she's still down. Bubba needed two attempts. This is the first time I can remember when both girls went to bed, and I didn't get a hug from either (being at the lake doesn't count because I'm not at home). I don't like it. The last time I was at home and our eldest wasn't here overnight I didn't sleep. It was so uncomfortable, and my insomnia ran riot.

TUESDAY 6 JUNE
11.01PM

Things are manic. The pace isn't slowing. Ever seen Charlie and the Chocolate Factory? (The glorious original; not the other one…?) My life currently reminds me of the boat trip in the chocolate room.

Speaking to my friend tomorrow for some precious, professional advice - I hope he makes it. And it looks like he will;

eventually. If wealth was determined by hard work alone, he'd be minted.

These digressions are symptomatic of my head not being right. They might make amusing, even interesting reading. But it's not funny for me. And at least it shows how quickly your head can become messed up.

WEDNESDAY 7 JUNE
8.00PM

My friend was harsh; but honest - which I admire and respect. He said a memoir wouldn't work because people haven't heard of me. Honestly? I don't agree. I think if you have something genuine, interesting and important to say. People will read it. But professional insight is so valuable, it gives me a base to build from, and I'm even more determined to make this work now.

THURSDAY 8 JUNE
VERY LATE

I'm still thinking about the book; my life, my plans and dreams. It's dawning on me how hard this is going to be. But I've got to keep going, not give up. No point spluttering on your death bed about regrets is there?

FRIDAY 9 JUNE
10.00PM

My wife had stuff to do so I took the girls to soft play. It was fun - not massively relaxing though. I was just trying to put my feet up. We've got a busy weekend ahead. I'm getting anxious again - the plans and the structure - the insane feelings of claustrophobia driving me absolutely nuts. Feeling like a caged animal, like an explosive ready to detonate. I'm already thinking I'll be back at work and won't have had any time to relax. I feel like I'm suffocating. I'm feeling manic - so selfish.

SATURDAY 10 JUNE
LATE - AGAIN

I'm tired and irritable. Such a long day but there was no choice. Our eldest had another party; three hours of non-stop pass the parcel and trampolining. I was struggling socially; savage and isolating paranoia. I wasn't that I didn't want to speak to people, of course I did. I just couldn't. Or even make eye contact. I wish I hadn't left my shades at home. They make hiding so much easier; and less obvious.

We only had a couple of hours until Nanny and Grandad arrived. I asked them to come early. Giving us more time to get ready - and time there on our own. My wife looked stunning; a beautiful, radiant lady. Sitting in the pub garden before everyone arrived I felt so good. No distractions; just precious time with each other. All the stress and struggles are worth it for these moments aren't they...?

SUNDAY 11 JUNE
9.50PM

Lucky, I didn't drink. My wife went to a boot fair, so we went on a double buggy adventure. Our 'adventure' ended up being me pushing the girls around the nearby lakes and parks. It was lovely; but when we got home I was knackered. They were full of energy.

My claustrophobia and feeling of being trapped is getting worse. I cannot stand having plans all the time. Feel like I'm going to explode if this carries on too much longer. I don't like the feelings and emotions building inside me.

MONDAY 12 JUNE
AT MY WIT'S END

Can't remember how many times our eldest woke up - I basically had no sleep. I went to work and must've looked a disgrace. Everyone commented. I couldn't face looking in the mirror. I'm not sure what was worse, the thought of seeing what was looking back at me, or the fact I genuinely didn't care about myself at all.

Took our eldest out on her bike – it was fun; but my tank was empty. She's really gaining confidence. It's a lovely sight. I didn't finish cleaning until after eight o'clock. Then had to eat; but she was off again before I'd even eaten - *at my wits' end...*

TUESDAY 13 JUNE
9.05PM

Work's going okay. My wife picked me up. I jumped in the car with cream cakes - needless to say, I was the hero! Our eldest is still very tetchy though. Nights are hard. I've mentioned controlled crying again. My wife is not impressed; and thinks she's poorly. It feels like she's becoming more like me every day. I don't have many good traits, but as long as she doesn't get any of my unpleasant or destructive ones I'll be happy. Bubba's teething is getting worse - if self-harm could take my girls' pain away - I'd already be bleeding.

WEDNESDAY 14 JUNE
GRENFELL TOWER

One of the most tragic events of modern times... It's so sad. You can't even begin to imagine the pain and suffering the victims and their families have been through. There's really nothing that can be said. My heart goes out to everyone affected. And to the amazing emergency services who did their best to help everyone affected. The images on the television were heart-breaking. Homes destroyed, lives lost, families decimated.

It makes you feel so grateful for everything you have.

THURSDAY 15 JUNE
8.35PM

Decided on a change of angle with our eldest... Normally when I get home she gets excited. Starts bouncing off the walls and gets told off. Then goes to bed early and has restless nights.

So tonight, instead of sitting on my big fat arse I took her scooting. She had a lovely time. We came back and watched her favourite programme 'PJ Masks'. And I decided to let her stay up a bit later; just fifteen minutes. But when she went to bed she immediately seemed happier and calmer. And went straight to sleep - a fluke? Perhaps; but I'll try the same thing tomorrow. So, we'll see. As parents we cling on to these little victories, don't we?

It's such a nice evening. I might go and sit in the garden with a beer... So, go and do whatever makes you happy... Even if it means putting this down!

FRIDAY 16 JUNE - MONDAY 19 JUNE
AT MY WITS END *(AGAIN)*

No medication, no self-esteem. It's not rock bottom. But it's close. I've lost four days - loads has happened. But I've just been the shell of a man. Taking nothing in; I have no recall. No memory - blank. I could have been in a coma; or on a booze bender and had a massive black out... Think it's known as saturation point - tired but can't sleep. Hungry but don't want to eat. Gasping, but don't want a drink. Exhausted but can't sit still or get comfortable. It's scary, whatever it is. If you've ever felt like this, or are feeling this now, speak to somebody; anybody. Just please, please, don't suffer in silence. Not like I did.

TUESDAY 20 JUNE
ON THE BUS

I know it's bad. Goes against everything everyone has told me - family; my doctor and my therapist. It's not even rebellion. It's not that I think I'm better either. I know I'm not - and that I'll probably have challenges for the rest of my life. People say; *look into yourself for the answers.* What if you can't find one? The mania is coming back. But the highs and lows seem to be lasting longer - more emotional, moody, more intense, less and less control.

Now I'm on the sofa. I'm starving. But the thought of food is making me sick. I'm on fire. The shakes are so bad. It's scary how quickly my thoughts; and state of mind change.

WEDNESDAY 21 JUNE
11.00PM

The last two weeks have been the hardest for a couple of tears. I just mistyped and wrote tears instead of years. Ironic - there have been plenty recently with my eldest. When she's upset I cry inside... Sound wet? If you think that's the case maybe you need to look in the mirror. Unless you're afraid of what will be looking back at you. Sound harsh? I said this might be uncomfortable. But it's when we're in these tough, dark places, backed into corners, that we learn most about ourselves.

Bubba isn't any better either. Nothing we can do. Cuddles and unconditional love all round - no way I can go upstairs now. I don't like the sofa, it's lonely. But I need some sleep. My wife must get lonely too. I feel guilty about that because it's my fault. If I wasn't mentally ill, I'd need less sleep. And could handle all the wake ups better, broken sleep and difficult nights easier.

Some of these feelings I'm writing about and experiencing for the first time. I don't know where they'll take me. But for now, I'm taking myself to bed (the sofa).

THURSDAY 22 JUNE
8.00PM

Every time I've sneezed or coughed I've had to sit on the lavvy. Inevitable, I suppose - getting sick whilst looking after the sick. My rear end is on fire. You can't rest either with two girls at home. Every time they bundled me I thought I was going to have an accident. Go ahead, laugh! But it's like getting a football kicked in your bread-basket. Everyone else struggles not to laugh while you're in trouble...

Possibly my most physically humiliating entry yet...

I said this would be uncomfortable...

Promise kept.

FRIDAY 23 JUNE
10.09PM

About six o'clock I started to feel better, so had a massive munch up - my problems with food resurfacing. No off switch - still eating when I felt sick. Shortly after finishing I had to pay another trip to the bog...

I'm worried about being off work. And paranoid about what will happen.

We had to cancel speech and language therapy. But she's been better the last month. We're finding the techniques are working:

- Asking fewer open questions
- Not finishing her sentences for her.
- Giving plenty of time to reply
- Not rushing
- Not talking just to fill time. Quality over quantity communication

It's challenging but so rewarding. Nothing can prepare you for the emotions you feel as a parent. We learn as we go. But that's the fun isn't it?

First day we've all felt better. I can fart with confidence; walk and eat normally. Isn't it crazy how the simplest things can offer such immense pleasure? I cancelled my fishing trip as loads on - hate doing that. It stresses me out.

We went to my wife's nephew's eighteenth birthday party. He's such a lovely guy; a gentle giant. But he also has conditions that mean he needs constant care. I love him. He's amazing. He lives his life and enjoys it to the fullest. Of course, there must be hard times. But his family are amazing too. I've enjoyed watching him grow up since me and my wife got together. I think people could learn a lot from him; including me. But we're all so insular. And guilty of losing perspective; I know I am.

In the evening we went on to the Midsummer Night's Feast - an evening of local food beer and music. I'd been there for five minutes and bumped into my head of department. Fuck sake. I'd been off sick for two days; then he sees me in town. *WHY? WHY ME?* Paranoia engulfed me. I had to go get a beer. I needed somewhere to hide, to regroup. It was my worst nightmare. The scary thing is though, while paranoia was crippling me, he probably didn't give it a second thought. I don't feel well.

SUNDAY 25 JUNE
9.00PM

We started making plans for our week off. By lunchtime my head had totally lifted. It wasn't bad when I woke but it was there. A dull reminder of alcohol's come-down. It's a strong, dangerous drug. That's why I often refer to it as that. Not a hangover. You drink? Then you'll know what I mean. The crazy thing is that when I was in my very dark and heavy drinking phases I used to use alcohol to cure a hangover. And that can be a very slippery slope...

Anyway, mid-afternoon my mother-in-law called. Offering to pay for us to go to Butlin's... Our first family holiday; two nights away! We accepted graciously and immediately made our first mistake... Telling our eldest; who then didn't want to go to bed. She was so excited... I just wanted some peace! The selfishness again; you see...?

BUTLIN'S - DAY ONE
LATE

More manic than we could have ever predicted! Filled with chaos; fun and full-on meltdowns...

Last night my wife pretty much did all the packing and preparation. That's always the case. I'm useless - partly because my mental health affects my very short-term memory and partly because I'm a useless twat. Aren't most men when it comes to this stuff?! She's a saint. I'm not sure I'd even put up with me... No, I am sure, I'd never put up with me...

I was uptight though because our eldest wouldn't stay still. Not her fault. I can't afford to pay for a holiday myself; my fault. I couldn't drive there; my fault. I was tired; (probably) my fault.

We went straight to the aqua park. After two hours she went ape. A total meltdown - tired, angry, short-tempered and over stimulated.

Dinner was a disaster. I left with the girls, so my wife could eat. Then later that evening she picked up a bug. By half-nine all the ladies were in bed. I went and sank a few cold ones in the hotel bar and processed things. I didn't eat; again.

BUTLIN'S - DAY TWO
10.00PM.

Much less stress and much more fun. Theme park, arcade then huge soft play area. Then Mr Maker, the CBeebies star. Not fun, not for adults anyway. Play Doh live; a trippy three-dimensional stage show, great for adults. The girls both absolutely loved it. Our first proper family adventure... Our restaurant got evacuated just as we sat down. Just our luck - we take it everywhere. Incredible.

I'll be lucky to get much sleep tonight, but I'm happy. I feel much more at ease; less knotty.

WEDNESDAY 28 JUNE
HOME - THE FALLOUT

The departure wasn't stressful. The morning was nice - relaxing and great for my mental health. I'm smiling thinking about the day; the video reel in my head spinning, recalling events - the tears; the strops; the smiles; the exasperation; the laughs, the cuddles and the jokes. Everyone's now in bed.

That trip was good for my soul.

It's been grumpy all day - the house and the people in it. We played games and watched TV; but are finding it hard re-adjusting to normal life. I had flashbacks to all my travelling and trips away...

(I flew to South America to travel with my then girlfriend and her best friend. After landing in La Paz we went to the hostel. The following evening, we went into the town for a look around. As we walked down the road two people approached a man from behind. They pushed him to the ground. And a man walking towards him caught him. They then tied his arms and legs together and gagged him, before dragging him up an alleyway... In broad daylight; only metres away from us - nobody batted an eyelid. We immediately went back to the hostel. Bolivia is a staggeringly beautiful place though; utterly spectacular.

I didn't see much of Chile. But what I did was simply amazing. Iquique is a beautiful seaside town in the north of the country. We spent a few days there, sun worshipping.

About half a mile off shore; there was a run of buoys people kayaked along. Swimming alone, I decided to go exploring beyond them. It was amazing, so remote. It was awe-inspiring.

I quickly attracted the attention of a pack of sea lions. I assume they were wild. After a few minutes they started to come close. Eyes fixed on me. It was exhilarating. Then they circled me; four of them - and started to dive. I stayed still; captivated by their performance. I could have been killed; snapped like a twig. Initially I felt scared, but then calm – I felt they had no intention of harming me. Ten minutes later I swam back to shore. I was buzzing. It was a once in a lifetime experience in a spectacular place).

And then thoughts about how I managed when I got back - yup. Booze and wild behaviour combined with idiocy, ignorance and rebellion. I'm sure somebody once wrote something about spots and a leopard… Change…? It's over-rated. Do we change when we marry? Are we supposed to?

What do you think? Did you change when you got married? Maybe you got divorced because one of you didn't change?

Did I, or have I changed?

Four things that have changed me; and I mean properly? Meeting my wife, the birth of my two girls and my mental illness…. Yeah, it's not always a nice world. But I'm comfortable with it. It's okay for us to talk about it. Breakdowns happen… But fortunately, many people do get better. Or get well enough to cope with everyday life. And enjoy it.

THURSDAY 29 JUNE
10.00PM

A trip to the wildlife park I wasn't up for. I'm still having the ups and downs. Mood swings people describe them as... I prefer mood shifts. Swings sound very unstable. Maybe I am? It's not that I don't want to accept it; more that I don't know if that's correct. But you can't hide from yourself, can you? Not if you want to be healthy.

Maybe that's the point; I'm hyper emotional and so sensitive. So that's a key factor of my life and mental health.

My temper was short but that's just because I want to go fishing now... After the appointment tomorrow, I'm off. So is my eldest; to Nanny and Grandad's.

FRIDAY 30 JUNE
6.30PM

The speech therapy appointment was good. They're happy with everything, and us. We just need to persevere. Stability is the key...

It's hot; I can feel my skin burning. The lake is packed. I go fishing to get away from people. Not to be surrounded by them. Fishing is part of my therapy. Some people just think it's a camping trip.

I'm drinking rum in the sun. My shoulders are dropping - two types of warmth. One splendid, one blended.

I'm relaxed but the guilt is creeping in. It always gets me in the end. Guilty I'm here and that my wife is at home with our Bubba. Guilty I've asked my parents to take out eldest. From the outside it looks like it's all about me. That's how it looks to me too; and feels. But I've no mania or paranoia. Sometimes I can't stand myself or my own company. Today I'm at ease.

I know the last few entries have been an emotional blast. It's a lot to feel and write. But I hope you're identifying with some of this? And that you can see you're not alone - and that whatever you feel, and however scared you are, it's okay to be.

EIGHT. (NO) MEDICATION

SATURDAY 1 JULY
SUNDOWN

My bowels moved more than my body today. No guilt though. I'm recharging; regenerating and it's absolutely needed – for everyone.

I'm glad I've barely seen anyone. Not in the mood to talk to people or even feign interest when listening to them. The eye contact thing again. No ability to look anyone in the face.

Back to the ladies tomorrow...

SUNDAY 2 JULY
10.05PM

I woke up exhausted, frustrated and ratty. Not even hungover; just washed out. It's not supposed to feel like this. Now I feel cheated; like it was a waste of time. I wonder; when I feel like this, if I'm being punished for leaving my family - arranging babysitters just so I could go fishing - for wanting free time; for needing free time. I hate being manic like this. Thoughts pulse through me before I can process them. There's nothing I can do - and normally includes all the death anxiety... So hard to hide and manage at work.

Even the slightest little thing pisses me off. I used to be so easy going. I still am to a degree; but when I'm dark my fuse is short. And things grate me. I wish I knew when that started. My breakdown was basically a year ago – it feels like a decade. So much has happened. Phases where I knew I was going backwards, times when I was on the crest of the wave. But felt too 'up' if that makes sense. That's the mania.

When people look at us they have no idea what's going on inside. Unless we talk.

MONDAY 3 JULY
9.30PM

A stressful and draining night - girls restless; and I can't sleep. The mania currently lasts up to an hour at a time. The insomnia can be two weeks or a month. If you suffer these conditions, you'll know - wide awake in the dark; staring at the ceiling. And your brain won't switch off. Sometimes I have the television on and lay with my eyes shut. Sleep? No chance.

I'm more honest with my wife now - the downside? She worries. The upside...? Hopefully it helps her understand me better and makes us stronger. Either that or she'll conclude I'm a liability and head for the exit... I'd never blame her if she did. If you're sitting reading this wondering what the next step is? If you can be honest with just one person, that's the first step to better relationships; and better health.

Day by day our eldest surprises me more. Bubba's teething is getting worse. And nights are difficult (again), wake ups; more frequent. My wife gives our home so much. It feels like all I contribute is grief. I'm not sure how much more I can take, how much lower I can go...

No mirrors for a while.

TUESDAY 4 JULY
9.30PM

Not really feeling anything. Emotionally bereft; but maybe it's a good thing. Nothing is stressing me out. But nothing is making me happy either.

Not caring about sleepless nights. Just going through the motions; both at work and at home. My wife knows it and can see it. But I'm trying.

It's not *normal* (whatever the fuck that means anyway) to feel like this is it? But how many people don't admit it? And simply get on with it? Maybe you do? Ignorance, and denial... It's easy isn't it? But it's dangerous and damaging. And I'm talking from personal experience. If you're having problems I'm sure they'll be affecting relationships at works, at home, with family and with friends. It did me. And still does.

Not feeling as numb. My nerve endings are tingling again. I remember just before I started therapy my doctor talking to me about strong drugs called mood inhibitors. So, I did some research, and this is exactly what they do; numb your nerve-endings and stop you feeling anything - it petrified me. My emotions and feelings are what define me, you, all of us –it's what makes us unique. And a course of pills can just wash all that, you, everything; away.

Now there are so many people with far worse conditions than me. Whose lives are saved and changed by such medication. I count myself lucky that my conditions, although debilitating every day, can, currently, be managed by therapy – and strong herbal antidepressants. Just about.

Some days are rough; I'm not going to lie. But the payoff is the good days; the positive feelings. The love and warmth I feel from my two little ladies. Feelings of awe whenever I'm around my wife; and the days I feel like I'm a good dad and husband. I wouldn't swap them for anything. No matter how bad and painful the bad days are.

THURSDAY 6 JULY
11.30

It's been a long week at work and not one I've enjoyed. I've had very bad paranoia; struggled to make eye contact with people;

or wanted to. The world is flying by around me. I'm in my bubble, not even trying to get involved or keep up.

The evening was nice, just chilling with my ladies - simple, quality and priceless family time. When you work to live it makes it all worthwhile doesn't it? Single? Enjoy going out on the town! I'm not jealous. One bit. Sense the tone. I'd love to have a blow-out. The type where you wake up still hammered. Then check your phone for signs, or messages of regret, or stupid behaviour.

I'm thirty-eight. Should people of our age have grown up by now? But maybe we shouldn't. Surely everyone is entitled to let their hair down? My problem is my hair has rarely been up in the last twenty-five years. Looking back, it's scary; I've lost so much, but still have everything a man could want. Well almost everything.

So, for now, here's the middle finger to societal convention. I'm having some rum. If I fancy a snifter, I'll have one. Cheers.

FRIDAY 7 JULY
10.12PM

Proper family time... But too hot for children - luckily our south-facing garden is big enough for a paddling pool. You see? Nice house and well-paid job. A beautiful wife and amazing children, a big family and good friends... But sometimes all I feel is loneliness, frustration, sadness, isolation and pain. Sometimes we never see all the good things.

They say love is blind... Add mental illness to that. It doesn't matter what you've got or who you are. Everyone is vulnerable. Everyone can be susceptible. Nobody is immune.

SATURDAY 8 JULY
JUST BEFORE MIDNIGHT

Last night was rank. Everyone woke up unhappy; I was moody and had barely slept. The girls wanted to play... Me? I wanted to sleep. It's not their fault. But I wasn't up for it; and was snappy and out of order. I could see it, but it's not that I couldn't care, I just couldn't control it.

Our eldest needs juice. It's no surprise, she needs to keep hydrated. At least I wasn't asleep. It's much easier this way. Sometimes I'm grumpy when I do night feeds etc. I shouldn't be. Fatherhood was my choice. It's our choice. Nobody chooses to be brought into this world. It's our responsibility to look after children when we do. End of.

SUNDAY 9 JULY
LATE AGAIN

Work tomorrow. It'll follow three nights with barely any sleep.

We tried another family trip. A little fun fair near our house... It was hot. And rubbish. No good for our children so we left pretty much straight away. The weekend's been a wash out. Or burn out. The girls have struggled with eczema. Another unpleasant thing I wish they hadn't inherited from me.

My wife has been okay, although she gets flustered. But who doesn't when looking after two children in extreme heat?

I need sleep - and my medication.

MONDAY 10 JULY
9.30PM

Been feeling very lonely; not something I've experienced for a while. Think it's the self-imposed isolation at work. Not really seen any of my mates for a while either - sad really.

It was nice to get home. (Although everyone was tired. And the house was a dump). So much love and warmth; it makes you smile without having to think. I plonked my arse on the sofa and was immediately bundled by a tidal wave of squeals and hugs. My wife looked tired but beautiful.

It's nice to sit in a quiet house. Although then I'm alone with my own thoughts, which are currently very dark. They're regressing and largely unpleasant. The dreams are back. Last night I was gunned down near my house. - absolutely riddled with lead.

TUESDAY 11 JULY
8.30PM

No disturbing night terrors last night. But that's because I barely slept. But things are good at home. I've been totally honest with my wife about my problems. Opening-up is hard. If you're struggling I can absolutely assure you that you're not alone... But I'm letting her in.

We're thinking about another holiday – I'm facing the the fact I can't afford even a basic holiday for my family. It makes me feel worthless and low; but there's nothing I can do. I hate not being able to provide.

Nan doesn't seem to be any better. She's so thin. It's so sad.

Makes you appreciate getting home even more. The girls were tired, so we played some new board games. We're starting to get more family time like this. I'm sure it's helping our eldest with speech and language therapy. It's certainly helping me.

I told my wife to go to bed early. Just to try and have a rest. Bedtimes with the girls are the nicest part of my day.

Laying on the sofa; listening to the wind whistle. I can hear my heart beating. As well as feel it. I don't like it; don't like to be reminded about my fragile mortality; death anxiety again.

WEDNESDAY 12 JULY

LATE

My mania is almost uncontrollable. I need my brain and thoughts to slow down. Writing is hard. That's why this entry is so short. I need to put my phone down and sort my head out - too much going on and I'm unable to process anything.

THURSDAY 13 JULY
10.00PM

Our eldest was awarded her very first trampolining badge; a special moment! I puffed my chest out - the proud daddy.

Our little Bubba's development has exploded... She's now drinking follow on milk. Even more amazing she's in her cot in her own room. And liking it! She's waking up only twice; which is good considering she's teething. And eating proper food... Toast, egg sandwiches, ice cream, blended vegetables, yoghurt, custard to name a few things... Cheeky little monster!

The first glimmer of hope for a career in mental health - my new friend contacted me about doing some freelance work. It's not definite; and could go nowhere. But it would be amazing. I just want to help people. There's so much I feel I can do. Time will tell I suppose. I'm going to give this absolutely everything.

I'm having a cup of tea tonight. Not beer.

FRIDAY 14 JULY
8.30PM

I'm doing the monitor again. Last night it was two wake-ups between them. Our eldest went to Nanny and Grandad's so we only have Bubba tonight. Meaning my wife will have a couple of nights off - on the menu? Rest and sleep; watching crap television, whatever - just some time for her.

I've barely done any nights recently. But I've been unwell and needed sleep - guilt and paranoia again - it's a gut-wrenching and soul-destroying combination. It scrambles your brain and knots your stomach. I hate it. But they're invisible – If you don't tell people they only exist in your world.

SATURDAY 15 JULY
11.00PM

Our luck goes from bad to worse. Tried to tax the car... DVLA website said we had no live MOT cert! We forgot to renew because we've been so flat out with everything else. So, we booked it in. Guess what? Yup! Failed... More money we don't have. I feel sick... Why does this stuff always happen to us? WHY?! Mechanic quoted £400. I nearly puked and cried - simultaneously.

SUNDAY 16 JULY
11.45PM

First weekend for ages I've not drank. I still felt like I had a huge hangover. Punished for abstinence! But it'll do me good. It'd be nice to shift some of my beer gut. I look like a beer keg on legs.

The headache must be sleep deprivation. Doing nights can be a pleasure. The house is silent... I get to have a quick cutch and do a feed; then put her back down. Yeah, I often don't get back to sleep. But fuck it. We're a long, time dead, right?

Our eldest has been so much better since I changed my approach towards her. I still think stuttering and general grumpiness was mainly my fault. But I did, and still am, doing my best to change. And I feel better too. Not like I'm failing - like I'm a better father - and better man.

I've managed to start taking my meds again. I already feel calmer; but concerned about a dependency developing. I'm sick of having this shadow that renders me a totally different person to who I am when it's not there. My addictive personality will pounce on anything. Paranoia has been very bad for two weeks. Really hoping the meds will help.

Addictive Personality Disorder

An 'addictive personality' is a colloquial or informal term based on the belief that certain people have a particular set of personality traits that predisposes them to addiction and other problematic behaviours, such as drug abuse or gambling. Although it is a fairly-common concept, there is no medical or scientific definition of an 'addictive personality' or 'addictive personality disorder.

Addiction can be influenced by various factors in one's life, including social environment, family, psychology, and biology. Personality, which reflects the confluence of a number of individual traits, is one of these factors.

(Source: Recovery.org website)

I finally told my wife about my book and my plans. After seven months... She was shocked it's fair to say. I don't think she was angry, I explained it was because of my failure complex, and because I wasn't sure if it would be any good or what would happen. I've also suggested she starts reading it soon. So, if she has any objections we can talk about them.

MONDAY 17 JULY
8.20PM

A horrible day at work; I received notification from the court that I have permission to evict four people on the grounds of rent arrears... I felt guilty and low all day. And I'll probably feel like this all week. I'm realising I'm not a good fit for the job and department I'm in.

Yes. You can argue these homes will go to people desperate for somewhere to live, who'll pay their rent – but I still felt awful; I still do. Like I've failed. I've only evicted two people before. I felt like this for days afterwards on both occasions. I can't wait to wave today goodbye.

TUESDAY 18 JULY
8.45PM

No guilt. But my anxiety and paranoia complex are excruciating.

Our eldest has her pre-school booster jab tomorrow. I can't go. I feel sick in my stomach. I should be there.

My wife has been a bit under the weather - just need to be watchful. Don't want her burning out. She barely gets any free time. She's so dedicated. But it comes at a price.

Dad agreed with me. Nan is very thin. He thinks she's not eating. She's such a lovely lady; out of the old school - a diamond. I'm so sad. That's why I couldn't face seeing my grandad in state at their home. I want to preserve happy memories. You might think this is selfish? Don't care.

My head's mangled.

WEDNESDAY 19 JULY
11.53PM

Huge thunderstorm last night, I was woken by a bolt of lightning so bright it was like my wife had switched the light on. Girls slept through. Not much for me after about three o'clock.

Proper day at work; nailed it... Walking home I had a tired body. But a clear head. When I'm like this I see the world so differently. The difference shouldn't be so huge. But that's my mental health. And probably will be until I snuff it. I know my lot. And after thirty-eight years I'm starting to be comfortable with it.

I look into Bubba's eyes; smiling and chuntering away. Five months old - so much love; so much hope. Such huge hugs; so innocent. Every blink heralds a new experience; it's utterly amazing. I hope she'll always be as happy as she is today.

THURSDAY 20 JULY
OH, SO LATE

Had contact from my consultant friend about the possibility of another idea/project. It's both scary and exciting. I feel so vulnerable now a few people know what I'm trying to do. What happens if I fail? People will laugh at me. I'm petrified I won't be able to cope... Nothing I can do now.

Nights are tough and bending me out of shape. But I'm sleeping upstairs again.

I looked thinner in the mirror.

Speech therapy tomorrow... Our eldest is improving. Still don't remember the last time I took her to bed. I'm letting her make these decisions under no pressure. And letting her come to me when she wants to. It's so hard. And sometimes I want to cry. And sometimes I do. But my instincts tell me this is the right thing to do. No matter how painful.

FRIDAY 21 JULY
9.05PM

Speech therapy was good. We're doing well...

In the therapy they do two sets of filming - one with her playing with us both; separately. This is to evaluate how we are developing our strategies and techniques to help and support her. You know what was interesting during my session? She got up, spoke to the therapist (a lady) and then went and spoke to my wife for a bit. That's the first time it's ever happened. You know what? I was ashamed and embarrassed. Why? Because she didn't want to sit with me; I felt crushed.

The therapist said I'd done exactly the right thing.

Stone faced; broken heart.

Low self-esteem.

Having low self-esteem isn't a mental health problem in itself, but the two are closely linked.

Some of the experiences of low self-esteem can also be symptoms of mental health problems, such as:

- feeling hopeless
- blaming yourself unfairly
- hating yourself
- worrying about being unable to do things.

If lots of things are affecting your self-esteem for a long time, this may lead to a mental health problem, such as depression or anxiety. I found lots of information om the mind website, where you can too. I recommended it, it's excellent. Mind's President is Stephen Fry; a genius. And a wonderful example or how brilliant we are, and that we can achieve anything.

I feel more relaxed about this now - even though she stuttered a bit in my video. I'm sure it affected me more than it did her.

SATURDAY 22 JULY
9.00PM

Today was another watershed moment. Bubba's first family swim! She was so cute and absolutely loved it. It was lovely being in the pool altogether.

Took photos of her in the inflatable rubber ring our eldest used in the water when she was small. She looked identical. Old memories flooding back; new memories being created. My wife had so much fun. But no surprise she paid for it later - a busted back.

Just one beer today... It's been a good few weeks.

SUNDAY 23 JULY
8.40PM

Three weeks since I had a hangover. You don't waste any of your day and you sleep better. I also feel like I have more energy. But I'm realising what a large part of my coping mechanism alcohol was. And will continue to be. I don't think I'll ever be tee-total.

It's nice to prove I can do it. Normally I have one drinking night a week. It's an easy habit to slip into. Trust me. Years ago, I used to drink in the week. And go to work hungover. Self-regulation feels good. Hopefully my system is starting to flush itself out a little...

I had a lovely time with Bubba this morning. She's adorable - so cute and cuddly; my gorgeous little Beamer.

Selfish or acceptable?

For my thirtieth I planned a trip to a lake in Morocco. I didn't make it because I misread my flight time. Yeah. I know what you're thinking... Anyway, I sent a flippant message to my mate in Portugal asking if he'd be up for going for my fortieth; before I asked my wife. I received a positive response - so had to fess up. Not sure she was too pleased. Is it wrong? Do I have no moral compass?

I think I'm a relatively good dad, husband etc. I'm not down the pub at weekends and I do what I can around the house. I try my best. But is that enough? Maybe it's not?

Is it wrong to want to do this? The most worrying thing is that I have absolutely no idea. Surely, you're supposed to instinctively know? See the train of thought, the amount of questions? I don't have a clue. My mind is everywhere, and nowhere.

What a manic mind dump. That was rushing out of me. My heart's slowing. My pulse is easing. I feel less agitated...

And breathe.

No teeth relief.

It's bad. Bubba's cheeks are red and swollen. She's in pain but smiling through it. Waking up loads through the night, but of course she will. It must be agony.

Our eldest has been so good lately; I'm so proud of her. But she still seems to have batteries lodged somewhere - no off switch. She just loves life; and lives absolutely every minute to its fullest.

I've stopped taking my meds again. I need to make time... But it's the co-dependency again. I'm trying to fix everyone else – trying to make everyone and the world better - and ignoring my own needs. I need to redress the balance a little, but without bringing on the guilt complex. That and the mania cause me the most sleepless nights. And have done for some time. Ever been in the position where you think about absolutely every possible outcome of everything you say and do before you do anything? Petrified of every reaction to every action you take? It's painful and draining. But if you feel this way or ever have? I understand.

WEDNESDAY 26 JULY
MIDNIGHT

Entries are getting later and later. Bubba's wake-ups are more frequent. I'm flying at work, but things are beginning to wind me up, agitate me; test my patience. Micromanagement erodes my motivation.

Some of the things my girls come out with just make me well up. I do seem to cry more than I used to - at little things too. That'll never change now. This is me. I've got so much work to do, outside work. Need a battle plan; and some luck. Then I'll have half a chance.

THURSDAY 27 JULY
5.30PM

I had a chat with one of our directors today. Mental health among staff isn't something that many organisations seem to be focusing on. I said I'd like to be part of creating a model which could be taken, with pride, and shown to other sector leading organisations.

For the first time in years I want to be a success. And believe in myself.

FRIDAY 28 JULY
10.00PM - EXACTLY

Swimming is now the routine. We all go. I hate the indoor pool - makes my asthma flare up. The girls love it. Bubba just kicks and splashes the whole time. She always finishes early, exhausted but happy! Our eldest wants to be in the 'big girl pool' as she calls it. Doesn't realise if she jumps in her feet won't touch the bottom! A situation where her fierce independent side doesn't help any of us... But she needs to keep hold of that. Keep hold of her individuality.

Crazy the price. Fifteen quid for a family; sometimes having to explain 'Mummy and Daddy don't have enough pennies' makes you feel a total failure. It's the look of sadness on a child's face.

SATURDAY 29 JULY
11.36PM

I'm using mirrors. My clothes aren't so tight, and my face is looking less haggard. Not heavy under the weight of my hang ups and conditions - except one... My eldest's stutter is still bad... But it's getting better slowly...

Every day I wake up I hope it's gone. I'd give a limb to banish it forever. Irrational guilt... Is one of the things that never truly leaves me. At its worst it's emotionally crippling - but now? It just makes me wish I was a better man than I am.

SUNDAY 30 JULY
8.47PM

Absolutely dreading work... Groundhog Day was a bad film. It's worse.

My ankle is a problem. Girls are giving me the run-around. My eldest knows I'm struggling and taking full advantage. I got some Codeine - says on the box *Only take for three days. Can cause addiction.*

Brilliant... I'll have to be careful - the paranoia.

After a play, my eldest dashed off running for the toilet. I limped after her - in my sandals; and agony. I tripped, made a dive and rugby tackled her to the floor.

She wasn't far from the front door, and the road.

NINE. DEMONS RETURNING

MONDAY 1 AUGUST
8.49PM

Very low this morning... Didn't want to leave my ladies. It upset me – I just wanted to stay cocooned in the house.

Arrived at work feeling sick; I was really missing home. I had the shakes - stared at my screen all day; struggled to pick up the phone. I don't think I said a single word to anyone around me. It was lonely.

I was welcomed home by three tired, ratty and grumpy ladies - tried to squeeze in a few hugs... But nobody was in the mood. Everyone wanted to go to sleep. I just wanted my dinner. Oh, and five minutes peace...

I'm not greedy.

TUESDAY 2 AUGUST
9.00PM

I have a sleep hangover...Think I'd feel better if I'd been quaffing rum all last night...

I've still not sorted Bubba's Christening. I loathe myself. We've now also got an application for free childcare. Not done.

Jungle garden needs taming. Not done. It's my window into next week. My week off…

My evictions are next week. I feel like I've failed our residents. Maybe I haven't done enough to try to help? It's a dark place.

Hopefully have my X-ray Thursday, then off fishing. My tension heads are bad. And I must be unbearable to be around – probably better off out of everyone's way.

WEDNESDAY 3 AUGUST
PAST MIDNIGHT

I'm clock watching. The hands are racing. Hours of possible sleep are rapidly decreasing. Nothing you can do when insomnia is in town. I'm just wishing my eye-lids would start to drop. My shoulders are rigid. My head stretched and fizzing.

We all function on auto-pilot, sometimes don't we? You just do what you need to do. It's reactive, right? There are loads of rubbish euphemisms. That's where I am. Making sure Bubba is fed, our eldest is settled and my wife rests when she can. Things are feeling more settled, so it's easier. We're trying to eat more together, especially at weekends. We're also continuing with the techniques from the speech therapist. She has good and bad days, but thankfully more good.

THURSDAY 4 AUGUST
10.57PM

I struggled to get out of bed.

Our eldest didn't want me to go to work; which made it worse. She was reaching for a hug as I was going out the door. I couldn't look back. I knew I'd cry.... How bad is that?

My day was. Phone – computer – phone – computer. Then a pointless X-ray (pain had gone). Then home.

Fishing, right? Wrong. My wife picked me up. And wasn't well. I was furious - totally unjustified and selfish. But I couldn't control how I felt. And I hated it - as I did myself. I felt like I was going to blow.

She was very emotional. And then I said; *This always happens when I try and go fishing.* What the fuck was I thinking...? I was frustrated, angry, pissed off, suffocating... Even though my family needed me! I'm still feeling guilty. It's this kind of feeling that lead to The Edge (my poem). The self-loathing is indescribable and excruciating.

I didn't go fishing. I'm not a total bastard.

FRIDAY 5 AUGUST
9.30PM

Had the hump this morning... I watched the sun come up, but from the wrong location. My wife and the girls woke up feeling a little better, so I'd done the right thing, the only thing to do. But I had itchy feet - pacing, scatty and full of energy.

I truly believe in Karma and on the way to the lake I got mine. A bottle of ice-cold wine fell out of a bag, shattering on the floor. And when I tried picking all the glass up I sliced my hand, twice. Claret everywhere... Not the good kind.

Had a chat with my old fishing buddy about my mental health... And was so relieved it wasn't awkward. But I don't think it was ever going to be - just my paranoia running riot again.

I miss my three ladies loads. But I need to get myself back. In the state I was in yesterday I wasn't fit to be around my children. It sounds a horrible thing to say. But I must be honest with myself. If I don't, I can't get better.

I also need to be honest with you.

SATURDAY 6 AUGUST
TOO LATE: DAMAGE DONE

I was chilling out at the lake until I eventually decided to pack up. I got back at lunchtime and my wife was furious because I wasn't back earlier. Sometimes I feel like I can't do anything right. That's not her fault. It's my head that's gone...

Boot fair tomorrow morning. I'll have the girls - hopefully my head will be in a better place. And I'll be able to be the dad they want, and that I want to be.

SUNDAY 7 AUGUST
11.00PM

Woke tired but happy – a lovely morning. First with Bubba; we had loads of cuddles…We chilled and played, and she grazed all morning! She looked so happy. Big tummy; and big smile. Like the cat that got the cream. And pouch. And milk. And banana - she'll try anything!

And then...

The tornado arrived! Our eldest came back happy and exhausted. Then it was all about bundles, huge hugs and tales of her adventures. When I speak slowly, she slows down as well. It's much better. For a while we just played board games together in a little cuddle circle. Our eldest won, she always wins... Bubba second... And yup, Dada third and lucky to be last... The cheating blatant!

MONDAY 8 AUGUST
9.30PM

My body aches. I've got pins and needles in my arms and pains in my stomach and side. This is the first time I've addressed the most embarrassing of all my conditions - Hypochondria. Every time I get a problem I just assume its cancer. I think it's because there has been so much in my family. And my irrational fear of death...

The conditions I suffer from are:

*Asthma

*IBS (Irritable Bowel Syndrome)

Hypochondria

Low self - esteem and trust issues

*Anxiety and (manic) depression

Mania

Body dysmorphia

Co-Dependency disorder

Addictive personality disorder

*Paranoia and loneliness

*Insomnia

(*) Conditions I'm currently taking medication for

I understand myself a bit better these days. And find it a bit easier (it's never easy though) to ride the highs and lows; and to admit when I'm struggling. I don't hide as much as I used to. I'd encourage you to do the same. Being open is initially horrible… But slowly it becomes easier. And I'd never change anything about myself or my conditions. There's no need for us to feel we should. Everyone finds their equilibrium, eventually.

I hope you're on the way to finding yours.

TUESDAY 9 AUGUST

8.45PM

Holiday... Day two - it's all about the girls having fun. So...
The wildlife park in the rain! Everyone was tetchy, so we went
to the girls' second favourite place *The Pizza Restaurant*... They
shared lasagne and loved it!

My insomnia won't budge... I've had about four hours sleep
this week. It's scary how awake you can be at three in the morning when you've been up for twenty-two hours.

11.39PM

I'm wide awake. Trying to work out what's troubling me. I
can't figure myself out. But what I do know is that it's affecting
people around me - especially my wife.

My body will break soon

My head already has

My wife's resolve? Who knows...

THURSDAY 10 AUGUST

JUST ABOUT MIDNIGHT

What do you do when it's lashing down? You guessed it, take a
trip to an amusement park... Chase and Marshall (Paw Patrol
fame) were there for a meet and greet, so our eldest had to go!

I was still tired, but my head wasn't feeling so pressured. Earlier in the week it felt like someone had clamped it in a vice. I haven't felt myself for weeks. I'm contemplating going back to therapy. But won't, and can't, take any time off work. I don't want the stress of the absence management procedure.

But the day was about our eldest. She smiled throughout. Running everywhere... Full of enthusiasm; full of life... The mirror opposite of me... In some ways we're so similar. But I'm so pleased that in other ways we're so totally different.

FRIDAY 11 AUGUST
11.00PM

The wildlife park again; at least we're getting value for money! Our eldest knows the park so well; and already has a routine. It's a little autistic (which runs in my wife's family) - the structure, routine and memory... And when I tried to go off route only slightly? A full meltdown; screaming and tears... Legs everywhere - as soon as we went back on route everything stopped. Calm restored.

She loves the animals - but loves soft play and the swings more. It's great that she enjoys being outside so much. I don't want her to grow up a television or computer junkie - and as for social media? I'll be having proper words with her when the time is right.

Everyone is sleeping soundly after a long day. I'm sitting here with my thoughts; my anxiety. My mania and my insomnia - it's relentless. My eyes won't stop darting around. Thinking it would be easier if I was dead... I'm not suicidal. Just thinking that state of being would currently be easier than this.

Borderline personality disorder

Borderline personality disorder (BPD) is a type of personality disorder. You might be diagnosed with a personality disorder if you have difficulties with how you think and feel about yourself and other people; and are having problems in your life as a result

This description is from the Mind website, where you can find loads more information about this.

SATURDAY 12 AUGUST
YOU GUESSED IT... LATE

My wife and I fell out. Apparently, I'm always on my phone. I'm using it now to write this, so she probably has a point. But there are worse traits and fathers about than me. Now I feel like I'm not good enough. The self-loathing is turning my stomach.

I decided to take our eldest out. We went blackberry picking, then to the park near our house. She ate as many as she put in the bag and got juice everywhere!

Then we went to the pub on the way home. There's a huge garden. We played hide and seek; then barrel-rolled down the hills and had fizzy bubbles. It was one of the nicest three hours I've had for ages.

I'm still thinking about the argument. My paranoia, self-loathing and guilt are both off the scale.

I shouldn't be drinking...

SUNDAY 13 AUGUST
10.55PM

I give up...
    I'm contacting my therapist tomorrow...

MONDAY 14 AUGUST
10.00PM

Struggled to leave the house - almost didn't. I was honest at work; not sure how it was received. Some people still don't really know what to say or do. It's not their fault. Nobody at work really knows me so what do I expect? But after a while everyone just carries on with their work. We're too busy to do otherwise.

I called my doctor and text my therapist.

TUESDAY 15 JULY
9.00PM

Very bad and lonely day at work. I look and feel a state. I'm spiralling... My paranoia is reaching an unmanageable level; IS IT my fault I'm mentally ill? Am I a terrible person? Am I good at my job? What do people say about me behind my back, when I'm not there? I'm anxious all the time. I nearly broke down at work; felt like sobbing. But knew if I started, I'd never stop.

I feel like I want to scream; like the painting by Edvard Munch.

Although my head is so twisted and bent; it's more like a painting by Hieronymus Bosch.

Zero Gravity

When the blackness starts, and the shoulders drop
You wonder if the pain is ever going to stop,

The slightest wrong word causes such anger
The rage starts to boil and there lies the danger,

But out of the blue, your mood starts to shift
Your eyes widen, your shoulders lift,

Then out of nothing you're walking on air
And all those worries, no longer a care,

A spring in your step, akin to the moon
A feeling you hope, won't leave you too soon,

Ensuring that not a second is wasted
So grateful for how long the feeling lasted

Came home to a gorgeous wife and adorable girls... Our eldest wanting hugs and dashing towards me... Bubba giving me the standard arm waving. It melts my heart - every time.

But when you're unwell it sucks you in. It consumes you. You lose sight of everything - and sometimes everyone. Sometimes it just shadows you gently, sometimes it rages; causing insecurity and destruction. Sound melodramatic? It's far from it. I know what you are going through if you're suffering in silence.

WEDNESDAY 16 AUGUST
11.00PM

Darkness...

The time of night or the state of my head...? Both - it's getting harder and harder to leave the house. And work days seem to last forever. It's uncomfortable, sometimes excruciating. It's no way to live. Still not taking my medication often enough. It's self-neglect and self-harm; both on an unconscious and conscious level.

Strangely I've been getting on well with our eldest. The last time I was very unwell she kept her distance; probably because of the way I acted. This time I've been trying harder to be patient, kind and controlled. And it's working. I've started getting hugs again.

THURSDAY 17 AUGUST
PAST MIDNIGHT AGAIN

I went to my therapist - appointment done. My telephone referral is next Friday. I really didn't want to do this… But I've no choice… Right now, I don't know what is worse; denial or acceptance.

FRIDAY 18 AUGUST
6.54PM

A monster seaside trip! Our eldest's new favourite restaurant is a Brewers Fayre near the train station… Seating, soft play and a little cinema room. What three-year old wouldn't be in heaven. She was immaculately behaved. Surprise, surprise! We also did the Octopus (she calls it *oppowus*, it's adorable) garden, which is basically a huge indoor play centre - no wonder they slept on the way home. I'm trying to be more open about my mental illness now and making it clear no sympathy's required. I just don't want to answer 'fine' when people ask me how I am - when I feel so bad, so alone - so vulnerable; and so broken.

SATURDAY 19 AUGUST
9.52PM

A much-needed quiet family day; well morning anyway. We chilled out and our eldest showed me her new board games.

Bubba sat and watched… Until she got tired and flopped in her chair! It was nice to have some relief from daily life; albeit short.

Our eldest went to Nanny and Grandad's for the night. My wife and I had a bit of a cuddle on the sofa and chilled out. Bubba is never any trouble… She just likes eating and cuddles!

They went to bed early and I don't blame them. No point me doing that, so I had a drink. Or was it a few… Need you ask?

SUNDAY 20 AUGUST
8.30PM

Boot fair today. Attending only - with a massive hangover… Probably stank of wine.

We came back. And surprise, surprise our eldest wanted to go to the park. Or rather be pushed on the swing for ages. (I must have shoulders of steel). They're becoming more beautiful every day. Bloody gorgeous they are; just like their mum.

The girls simply have no off switch - games and bundles all afternoon.

I don't feel like I have an on switch…

One thing I do have is work anxiety. The last two weeks I've been dreading Mondays…

MONDAY 21 AUGUST
NEAR MIDNIGHT

Didn't see Bubba before I went to work - I hate these mornings. Sometimes I don't see our eldest either. I miss the hugs; the floppy cuddles, the doughy eyes. The mucky, breakfast filled kisses. The innocent mess... The mischievous glances...

Anxiety was terrible as I stepped out of the door. My clammy hand stuck to the handle. I had to prize it off... But it eased a little bit on the way in. Another thing I've noticed is I'm taking a different bus. One I know nobody will be on. Nobody I'll have to make eye contact with. Or horror of horrors, talk to...

It's sad. But at least I'm honest with myself. I know where I'm at. It's daily survival tactics. Whatever I need to do to make it through...

My wife can see I'm creaking... My mental illness feels more a part of me than ever. It must be so visible. I often wonder how unnerving and upsetting it is for other people too. Hello again, guilt, my old friend...

TUESDAY 22 AUGUST
10.30PM

Even though I'm struggling badly it's not affecting the girls. I'm managing to keep it hidden. I can do my stuff away from them. But going to the park most nights after work is helping - having time to relax and unwind. And our eldest loves it.

She's now asking me for a bedtime story and a hug at night. It's been a week or so now. But it makes such a big difference to me. The hugs - when she squeezes me, they're my favourite. You can feel the love. It's enough to make any man cry.

WEDNESDAY 23 AUGUST
11.51PM

I've started thinking about my appointment on Friday. I'm glad it's coming but I'm worried too. I don't want to be forced to change my medication. Or be signed off work. It's all-consuming. I can't focus on anything else. If you're thinking about therapy, this should not put you off. Yes, the very start might be uncomfortable and painful. But you'll hopefully slowly start to feel different. And realise what the potential benefits are. Just try and take one step at a time, at your own pace.

THURSDAY 24 AUGUST
8.45PM

Spoke to a couple of people about my illness today. I'm sick of telling people I'm okay when I'm not. The relief when I finished work was huge; even though the bus was late I could feel my shoulders going.

Our eldest had her friends around today. (My wife had some time with the mum's. It's great. I'm so pleased). The downside is when I got home she was asleep on the sofa, so I had to carry her to bed and tuck her in. I told my wife to go to bed too. And I had some Bubba time.

FRIDAY 25 AUGUST
10.00PM

My mental health assessment took about half an hour. I did it sitting in a hotel garden, drinking coffee, at about half nine.

Beforehand you fill out a questionnaire. The first part is on the first page of this book. The second part I'll share with you now, as well as my actual therapy - it's hard to do. It requires total, unequivocal honesty...

I hope this will help some people who read this - people who are afraid; who don't want to talk. Who are scared about what will happen if they seek help. Or how it works...

Over the last two weeks, how often have you been bothered by any of the following problems?

SCORING SCALE – 0: Not at all, 1: Several days, 2: More than half the days, 3: Nearly every day

- Little or no interest in doing things: 0
- Feeling down, depressed or hopeless: 2
- Trouble falling/staying asleep: 3
- Feeling tired or having little energy: 1
- Poor appetite or overeating: 1
- Feeling bad about yourself - or that you're a failure or have let yourself or your family down: 3 Trouble concentrating on things, such as reading the newspaper or watching television: 2
- Moving or speaking so slowly that other people could have noticed. Or the opposite – being so fidgety or restless that you have been moving around a lot more than usual: 1
- Thoughts that you would be better off dead or of hurting yourself in some way: 1

SCORE: 14/27

Over the last two weeks, how often have you been bothered by any of the following problems?

SCORING SCALE – 0: Not at all, 1: Several days, 2: More than half the days, 3: Nearly every day

- Feeing nervous, anxious or on edge: 2
- Not being able to stop or control worrying: 1

- Worry too much about different things: 2
- Trouble relaxing: 1
- Being so restless that it is hard to sit still: 0
- Becoming easily annoyed or irritable: 2
- Feeling afraid as if something awful might happen: 2

SCORE: 10/21

Choose a number from the scale below to show how much you would avoid each of the situations or objects listed below.

SCORING SCALE: 0: Never Avoid it, 4: Slightly avoid it, 8: Always avoid it.

- Social situations due to fear of being embarrassed or making a fool of myself: 1
- Certain situations because of a fear of having a panic attack or other distressing symptoms (such as loss of bladder control, vomiting or dizziness): 0
- Certain situations because of a fear of particular objects or activities (such as animals, heights, seeing blood, being in confined spaces, driving or flying): 3

SCORE: 4/24

People's problems sometimes affect their ability to do certain day-to-day tasks in their lives. To rate your problems, look at each section below and determine on the scale provided, how much your problem impairs your ability to carry out the activity.

SCORING SCALE: 0: Not at all, 4: Definitely; 8: Very severely/I cannot work.

- Work: 3
- Home management: 1
- Social leisure activities: 3
- Private leisure activities: 0
- Family and relationships: 4

SCORE: 11/40

The main concern for my therapist was that I have absolutely no self-esteem or self-worth. And the suicide stuff. My current overriding feeling is that everyone in my life would be much better off if I either wasn't around (i.e. moved) or 'took care' of myself. I'm extremely unstable, and unpredictable. I've also been subconsciously self-harming as well – by not taking either my asthma or mental health medication. It's punishment.

Secondary to this was struggling to leave the house. This; along with my insomnia, guilt complex, paranoia, co-dependency and other issues made me an urgent referral. And I was going to be hooked up with my therapist as soon as she was free.

Massive pre-wedding day too... My wife had her hair done and looked stunning afterwards.

Our eldest had hers done too. She has such classical, symmetrical beauty. Incredible really... That she came from me... Mine took twenty minutes. I hated being in front a large mirror - I kept my eyes shut.

The wedding

The weather was beautiful, more so the bride
The congregation so tearful, nowhere to hide

Beautiful speeches that lifted the tone
Surrounded by family but felt so alone
Felt so guilty and so full of shame
It's not about me, but changing a name

My cousin looking stunning, the spit of her mum
Her not being there made everyone numb,
Savouring her moment, back down the aisle
Feeling so hollow, I barely smiled.

Empty

It was a beautiful day; perfect for a wedding. Perfect for my cousin and her husband - just what they deserved, as did my auntie. Bless her. My uncle (her widow) is an inspirational, beautiful man.

The evening was fuelled by alcohol and emotion. Everyone felt it; the void. My auntie's daughters were amazing. Really did her and did my uncle proud. They are special ladies. Full of love and so strong. I love you all loads x

Mum too. She held up better than I thought - so proud of you Mum x

SUNDAY 27 AUGUST
8.00PM

Mouth like a horse's arse all morning...

So nice not having work tomorrow; and we did our obligatory park trip. Our eldest has a group of older girls she sees there. They're so nice and really make a fuss over her. She loves the big girls. And the ice cream van that comes to the estate next to the park!

I really enjoyed a football match for the first time this season. It's the little things. I don't ask for much. Or want for much. You don't need it do you?

TUESDAY 29 AUGUST
11.30PM

My nan's in hospital. It's either a reaction to medication, or the cancer - I've been told she's sedated and unresponsive. Poorly but calm. I don't want to do anything. I don't feel anything. I'm not thinking about anything, just existing...

What must it be like for my dad? And my nan, bless her. I just hope she's comfortable and not in any pain. And that she's also got people around her. If you're thinking *Well why's he not there then, the way he goes on?* I'm sad and scared. Nothing else I can say.

WEDNESDAY 30 AUGUST
9.50PM

It was the cancer. It's in her blood – doctor's said forty-eight hours... Tops...

My nan asked where my girls were; but I've decided not to take them. I want memories of great Nanny to be happy ones; of hugs and running around her garden. Not tubes, sadness and hospitals. I've no idea how to talk to our eldest about death. It's been on my mind since Nan got very poorly.

Guilt and self-loathing are back. And I'm not sleeping. My gut is knotted and wrenched. Nausea is constant. Am I doing the right thing? Will my family resent me? Will our eldest resent me when she gets older? It's horrible.

I hope you can see what this illness might be like for a loved one close to you who's going through a tough time - if this is you? Then stay strong. Things do ease.

THURSDAY 31 AUGUST
11.10PM

I spent all day waiting for the call, or the text... It never came... Existing again – it is crazy how we just waste passages of our lives, ignoring the fact that every second is precious, and life isn't forever...

I went fishing and set up in the dark. I'm sipping rum in total silence... Dark shadows everywhere.

Danny Boy,

You've been through so much; and some far worse things than me. But you were always available; and pestered me to talk to you about my problems - and helped me to see new ideas and alternatives in terms of my recovery and long term well-being. You offered as much advice and honesty as I was prepared to listen to. You should be so proud of how you've come through your challenges with such dignity. Thanks for everything.

To you, and ongoing good health,

Steve x

TEN. THERAPY (AGAIN)

My first therapy session... I turned up fifteen minutes early so I went and sat in the boozer opposite and quaffed a double-rum... I don't know why, I am what I am.

The questionnaire asks unpleasant but necessary questions. I was extremely manic. My therapist asked me *What do you want to gain from this? How do you want to feel?*

Fucking hell... It's like uncovering a bottomless pit. My eyes widened. I could feel my heart racing in my chest. The sweats... What do I want...? To not;

- Wake up every day feeling like a failure
- Feel like I don't deserve my wife, my children, my life
- Feel guilty about every single little thing I say or do
- Drag down the people around me
- Let my illness affect my three special ladies
- Have as many sleepless nights

And I want to like myself again.

I've concluded I'm not actually good at anything. I work to live. I have a job, not a career. Given the chance, nobody I know would swap places with me. Only Fools and Horses is a tenuous thread in this thing... There's a line from Rodney, I forget the episode, where he says, 'If there is such a thing as reincarnation, knowing my luck I'll come back as me!'

For about fifty minutes I barely stopped talking – an uncontrollable stream of consciousness - a flow of ideas and feelings with no order or logical links. She didn't even say that I smelled of booze; or ask me if I'd been drinking. Not sure whether she had picked it up. Or just chose to overlook it… At the end of the session I was tired and drained.

I was happy to get out of there...

I got back here, to the lake mid-afternoon - been drinking rum since then.

SATURDAY 2 SEPTEMBER
10.00PM

Massive storm overnight – my brolly snapped, and I woke up soaked, cold and angry. Why do I bother? A thought I often have. But rarely answer...

At least we had the Hop Festival as a distraction – our eldest's idea of heaven. Loud music, fizzy bubbles, Chinese food and a fun fair! Bubba loved it too! Bopping to the music, eyes darting around, excited arms and legs flailing everywhere!

I've had two meals in three days - but plenty of alcohol. I'm a state and a mess - mind, body and soul. It was nice to be out as a family, but I felt detached. I could see, and feel, my wife was worried.

Turns out there may have been a mix up with my nan's prognosis. And the medication administered by the doctors. She's now eating and likely going into a care home. My dad is confused and furious. I don't really know how I feel. It's a lot to take in…

SUNDAY 3 SEPTEMBER
11.00PM

Deja-vu

Full on again. But this time we were in a Chinese restaurant for the first time together. The girls were awesome. And ate loads! The smell of cooked food was making me want to puke. I couldn't manage a mouthful.

But it was lovely to be with my ladies, and I felt a little less detached.

I've started buying the odd scratch card. I need to be careful. I've been here before. I'm pretty good at controlling my addictive personality. But every now and then I have a little lapse; a splurge. Normally it manifests as binge drinking; certainly, in the last few years anyway.

It was nice to see the boys at lunchtime; although they gave me a roasting for not eating. I didn't feel comfortable around them. And they could see and feel it. It was horrible. And a clear indication of how unwell I am.

Bedtime was easy, the girls were knackered.

Having a nightcap… I'll be buried with one. A cremation would cause an explosion.

MONDAY 4 SEPTEMBER
10.00PM

No work... Beautiful! I needed a lay in. Not because I was hungover - simply because I'd barely slept for ninety-six hours. I slept until eleven. Our eldest went to gym class. I bailed because I'm a prick.

Felt hungry for the first time in a week so had a big feed and loads of fluid. Not booze. Not on school nights, remember.

Currently, I think whatever I do, or whatever decision I make, is wrong - a horrible place to be. Not liking yourself - I'm wondering how long this will last. It's awful isn't it? Being so uncomfortable in your own skin.

I don't want to hurt my wife. Maybe if she did meet someone else she'd be happier. She deserves the very best. More than I can provide. A better man than me...

Now I'm lying here wide awake. Work tomorrow. No chance of sleep. Head full of manic thoughts. Days since I last used a mirror? Not a clue.

TUESDAY 5 SEPTEMBER
APPROACHING MIDNIGHT

Nan is improving. No idea what's happening. That's why I haven't visited. Selfish bastard – yes, I know. But you don't have to like or fully understand me to get something positive out of this book.

A text I sent to my wife…

I'm so sorry. I never meant for your life to be difficult :-(It's one of the problems I have. I think you and the girls deserve so much better than me. I told my therapist I wouldn't blame you for kicking me out. I'll try and get better quickly. So, things get better for the three of you. Please don't feel guilty. There's nothing you can do. You're an amazing wife and mum. I'm currently the weak link. And I don't like myself because of it… x

WEDNESDAY 6 SEPTEMBER
9.30PM

The beard… So long; so prickly; so much white. Nobody in the house likes it; I don't hate it. But I can't shave without a mirror…

THURSDAY 7 SEPTEMBER
12.11PM

On the way home, we got stuck behind a bad car crash. Luckily the drivers and passenger seemed to be okay. I always feel so sad for the family members who are wondering why loved ones are unexpectedly late.

Took our eldest to the park after work to help her burn off some energy; and gave my wife a little break. She waits for me to come home now. It's nice; it's becoming our thing. I like us having a thing.

My wife has had to do the monitors for a couple of days because I've been very low after my appointment. I was expecting that. But not expecting it to last so long.

2.17PM

The dreams are starting again. This was a new one though. A group of vigilante paedophile hunters came to my house on my birthday. And told me I had twenty hours to hand myself in... And that I didn't want to know the alternative. I woke up and nearly spilled my guts all over myself.

FRIDAY 8 SEPTEMBER
THERAPY SESSION TWO

I felt flat. Dark, so down. Was dreading the session, I had no energy. No enthusiasm. No optimism. No fight. I could see my therapist was worried. I was just lost and afraid.

I'm so far off centre. So far away from the person I am; or used to be. My therapist was telling me I need to unpick my pain. And reconnect with that person. My answer...? I'm not even sure that person exists anymore. Maybe who I am now is the person I'll be for the rest of my life.

But if this is you, please consider this. Your illnesses have almost certainly made you a better person in some ways. It might just take you a little time to see it. Your life perspective will make you more understanding, empathetic, tolerant and loving, even when you're in the depths of illness and pain.

My therapist kept repeating about commitment. Was I committed? Would I commit to the course, the journey? To living my life? When I was sat in that room? I honestly thought 'no'. But I made myself say 'yes'. She didn't buy it; or believe me.

She was concerned I have few childhood memories until about the age of five. I thought it was just years of drinking wrecking my brain function. Turns out it's due to trauma.

After about half an hour we concluded I have zero self-worth and zero self-esteem - none. That's why I don't think I deserve life, my wife and the girls. And they'd be better off if I wasn't around (left or dead. Currently, the second option appeals to me more).

We ended by doing this iceberg analogy thing. You have the tip above the water. This is the five percent of you that people see, hear and know. The rest is below the surface. What they'll never know, unless you tell them. And it's broken down something like this:

- Level of consciousness
- The sub-conscious - feelings and emotions
- Unconscious - beliefs about self-worth
- Innocence - love, fear and images.

My problems are coming from my unconscious mind. But I'm totally conscious of my problems.

Walking out… That's the worst I've ever felt after a session. I just wanted to get hammered. Numb the pain. Forget.

Temporarily escape. Honestly? I was on the precipice, of jacking everything in... For about half an hour I walked up and down the high street, walking past the same bars, looking in the same windows. But stayed away.

I was in crisis. I called my wife and was honest. I went home. Her relief was audible and obvious.

I missed our eldest's speech therapy evaluation today. They said she seems good. But she'll stay on their books so if it gets bad again we can get an appointment quickly. That makes me feel a bit better about it. With a stretched NHS, we're so lucky to still have ready access.

It's the same for my mental health treatment. My therapist is not far from me. And every time I've referred and self-referred, it's only been a couple of weeks until I had my initial assessment. I'm so lucky

SATURDAY 9 SEPTEMBER
10.00PM

I felt hollow this morning - dark mood and heavy shoulders. Not liking myself. I honestly didn't think, or realise I was this unwell. I'm still not taking my medication. It's blatant self-neglect. That's what my therapist said. When I said I'd barely slept or eaten for five days. She said; *Are you trying to kill yourself?* I said *No*. But I suppose it all links into the same thing. And I don't think she'd ask that type of question unless she was worried.

At least we had a family day. Leeds Castle is like a sanctuary away from home for me - peace and quiet, long walks and fish-filled lakes.

I didn't eat; I ingested my calories through local alcohol; again.

The self-medication (myth) continues.

SUNDAY 10 SEPTEMBER
11.00PM

The house is coming down with something and making nights hard. Badly broken sleep for everyone. The girls are ratty and tetchy - they need hugs; and lots of them. I'm sure they can sense I'm not right. Our eldest has been hugging me extra tight. She's the most amazing and caring little girl. I don't deserve any of my ladies. These feeling are something I can't currently change - I hate being like this; prickly like a cactus.

MONDAY 11 SEPTEMBER
10.00PM

After a night of two hourly wake-ups and about an hour of sleep my body is getting used to this. My mind is warped and twisted already. But not having much sleep clouds your thinking and can make decision-making easier - because you don't feel any emotional connection to anyone or anything. Sounds horrible right? But I'm fine with people judging me as aloof, rude or ignorant. You do what you need to do to get through each day, right? Surely there's no way that it's just me? Be honest...

And do what you need to do to get by. This is about you, and only you. Only you can get the help you need and accept it. The power and capability for change and growth is within you x

TUESDAY 12 SEPTEMBER
11.11PM

Text messages I sent to my wife today. It was easier than talking face-to-face. Totally gutless, but totally necessary:

Things are starting to move with the book. I'm going to be starting a small research project soon. And already have some people ready to take part.I need to tell you one thing. The night before I left my wife, I tried to end things. Nobody knows about this. Not even my dad. I basically drank a litre of vodka, took a shed load of pills and slipped off to sleep. Not expecting to wake up. I did an hour later. Was violently ill; then as soon as I could I cleaned up and got the train to my dad's house. Don't worry. I've not had any similar thoughts for a while apart from one when I was ill last year. I'm sorry this is not face to face, but I just need to tell you. I'm just trying to be honest with you. It's just one thing at a time. But please don't worry. I'm talking about it with my therapist x

The reason I didn't speak to you last year was because you were not having a good pregnancy. So, I decided to take it on myself. It wasn't a rash decision. I tried to make the best decision for our family at that time. I'll have to tell my parents at some stage too...

I'm not brilliant. But I've been worse. One of the biggest problems is I have zero self-esteem and no self-worth. That's why my paranoia and guilt complex is so bad. I don't ever think anything I ever do for anyone is any good - or good enough. But that's my problem. Not yours. And one of the reasons I've gone back to therapy x That's also why I struggle to keep any sort of eye contact with anyone. Why I don't go out with my friends as much as I used to. And why I sometimes feel lonely even when I'm in a room with my family and friends. It's not nice. But it's what I need to face if I'm going to get better xx But, none of this is your fault. You're amazing. It's me; and due to stuff, that happened to me, before we met (apart from one thing) which destroyed my confidence xx But, that wasn't your fault either!!!!! Xxx

WEDNESDAY 13 SEPTEMBER
11.55PM

I feel a little better opening-up to my wife; but so guilty I've burdened her. She doesn't need this. My guilt complex tears me in half. On a daily; even hourly basis. One of the reasons I don't like myself. My therapist asked me to try and start using mirrors again. *Not yet. No chance.*

The girls are sleeping terribly. I've been functioning on about three hours a night for two weeks - and eating even fewer meals per day. Don't remember the last time I had breakfast. Sometimes I make it just to give the illusion I'm eating. But just leave it in the kitchen. Or shove it in the bin. That's a big issue - and if this resonates with you? I suggest you talk to someone, because you're in trouble. The lies will likely also be prevalent in other areas of your life too - hiding other behaviours and problems. The earlier you can talk, the easier it will be.

Nan is getting worse quite quickly. I'm not going to see her. And neither are the girls. I've finally made my peace with this. No more guilt. Nothing to justify to anyone... Although I did explain this to my dad - out of respect really. He knew I was the same with my grandad, so he could see that this decision was for the same reasons.

We went out for dinner to one of our favourite restaurants. It was lovely. My wife looked so pretty - my beautiful blonde bombshell. The food was superb. My dear old friend really looked after us. He's a gentleman - a lovely guy. He also opened a special bottle of Metaxa to celebrate. Not generally my bag, brandy. But I make the occasional exception!

We had a nice chat, did some reminiscing. Talked about the future... Held hands... I've really missed our quality time. It's so precious; and we don't get enough. But I'm grateful for anything these days to be honest.

Text to Mum...

Hi Mum. I'm not going to go. I didn't see Grandad in hospital; or when he was in state at the home. It helped me to keep my precious memories - and to grieve. Nan is such a sweet, kind and gentle lady. I think seeing her right at the end would break my heart. I hope you don't think I'm selfish. But I'm comfortable with this decision. I'll also be arranging a babysitter for the funeral/ cremation. As it's not the right situation for children.

FRIDAY 15 SEPTEMBER
11.30PM

Our eldest only popped back briefly while Nanny and Grandad went to the hospital. Then she went back to their house. Our house felt so empty – our little Bubba just plays and rolls around on the floor. I told my wife to get an early night - to take the opportunity while it's there. She deserves it.

I'm not taking my meds. And have been nowhere near a mirror…

SATURDAY 16 SEPTEMBER
9.15PM

A
  Lovely
    Afternoon

Our eldest was invited to a birthday party. She's developing a nice little group of friends - as is my wife. I'm so pleased for them. I want them both to be happy and have nice people around them. Sometimes that doesn't mean me.

(For the most part I was lucky. There were lots of good people in my year at school. And at the local football club... Back then; me and two of my closest mates were inseparable. One Saturday evening we were messing around in my mate's room. One of them shouted 'catch' so I looked up. As I did the other turned the light off. Next minute a big plastic E.T. hit me right in the eye. The light being switched back on revealed instant swelling. They were rolling about laughing. I could only see out of one eye. And didn't play the next day... Most embarrassing sports injury ever... Bastards! Love you really you twats x But I was vulnerable even then.

I was gambling until about the age of twenty-five; always walking around with large amounts of cash on me, normally £300-£500. It felt nice. I don't remember this story because I was so drunk. But I've been told that one night, at a local bar, I was robbed in the garden - fleeced of all my cash. At least the alcohol meant I felt no pain; physical or emotional).

No updates on my nan. But any we do get will only confirm her decline. I've started grieving...

And my first glass of wine....

SUNDAY 17 SEPTEMBER
FOOD FESTIVAL

I was hanging this morning; could barely open my eyes. Not sure how much sleep I had. My wife needed time to do stuff, so I took the girls into town. Two wired girls, a double buggy and a hangover. That's a Hollywood film title right there...

Our eldest had a huge meltdown in town; just because she didn't get her own way. I put her over my shoulder, King Kong style and marched her back to the motor when my wife arrived - still going ballistic. Eventually she calmed down; so, we managed to enjoy the rest of the day.

Another weekend with very little sleep... Like shelling peas...

The bags under my eyes look huge.

Dark circles, dark mind.

Mum, Nan, great nanny Ann

My childhood memories
Her hair so white,
And love-filled cuddles
Holding me tight,

Down at the egg farm
Nan was my idol,
She was always so warm
The best role model,

Her Sunday Roast
A meal to behold,
Her famous rice pudding
Hot or stone cold,

I was always so happy
When she was around,
Her impact on me
Eternally profound,

She had her say
Took none of my cack,
Once I ran away
She sent me straight back,

An inspirational woman
A beautiful soul,
No need to be solemn
Her life was pure gold,

An unforgettable smile
That lit up a room,
We love you, Nan
We'll see you soon.

Tell Bunny we said hello x

Dad's also in the same hospital. Taken by ambulance after being knocked off his bike...

TUESDAY 19 SEPTEMBER
GRIEF

A terrible night. Mind racing; thoughts about Nan... Memories... Last time I saw her. Not seeing her again; flashbacks to my childhood. You couldn't make this up.

Nan passed away with nobody around her; horrible. You know the only solace? That she was in no pain, peaceful and comfortable. I hope she drifted off wrapped in a blanket of happy memories. Now I just need to get through the funeral. We'll only take our eldest to the wake. She'll just think it's a family party. What will I say if she asks where Great Nanny is? Absolutely no idea... But as long as manage not to cry I'll fudge it somehow.

Dad got hit by a car overtaking him on a hill. My wife drove passed and saw him lying in the road - and stayed until the ambulance arrived. I'm so grateful to her for that. He's out of the old school - which basically means he'll never wear a crash helmet. The doctors said he's lucky to be alive.

Nan was my last grandparent.

WEDNESDAY 20 SEPTEMBER
9.50PM

Barely slept; couldn't motivate myself. No interest in work; or food. Just thinking life is totally unfair. At least my dad is on the mend.

Cuddles from the girls and support from my wife is getting me through... The girls are incredible. Our eldest's hugs could stop wars. Little Bubba; well I just don't ever want to put her down. My wife is the constant. A beautiful metronome... Solid and dependable – unwavering and amazing.... my soul mate and the love of my life...

I always withdraw when someone close to me dies... I don't like being involved in the emotion and upheaval. I need to do my own thing; in my own way.

We all deal with death, bereavement and loss differently. You'll be different from everyone around you. It's a totally individual process.

I did even less than yesterday at work – absolutely no professional pride. I did spend some time talking to a lovely lady in my office who's going through similar things to me - it's nice talking to someone who understands.

I'll talk to my wife more; probably on the drive down to Butlin's when the girls are sleeping. She needs to know where my issues come from. After tomorrow's session, hopefully I'll take some small steps to unlocking things. But there's no quick fix, no guaranteed happy ending. This isn't a Hollywood movie. Real life doesn't work like that does it? But it's important you can see that, but also that taking things slowly works, and managing your expectations and being realistic about results and your improvement is essential.

At least I'm sitting here knowing I have ten days away from the office... But I'm *already* anxious about going back. It's insane. My head's a wreck.

Grieving... I can't work it out... Have I finished? Have I even started? Will I even start?

You'd think by the age of thirty-eight a person would have a tried and tested grieving process, a coping mechanism. Sounds clinical right? But it makes perfect sense - except I don't have one....

I still don't know if I ever grieved for my grandad. Or maybe I'm just dead inside...

My first day off - but my third therapy session... I'd rather be waiting for a tooth extraction. Maybe because I was afraid of what would be uncovered? Nobody really wants to dig up their past and reconnect with that pain, do they?

Everyone is still ill apart from me - I imagine I'll get it next week when we're away.

So...

Therapy...

I talked about Nan and Dad. How I didn't see my nan in hospital. Which is exactly what I did when Grandad died - I didn't feel guilty then or now... And I won't be answering to anyone or justifying myself. Why should I...?

My zero self-esteem and self-worth...

It's unquestionably linked to two things:

My treatment by women

Bullying as a child

The first one...

At college I was seeing a girl. She was my *first*. One day I went in early. And saw her with someone else on my course - *public humiliation.*

I went to France with college and lived with a beautiful French lady for a while. She dumped me - and started nailing a geezer on my course - *public humiliation... Again.*

A few years later I met another girl; a lovely girl. I travelled to South America to spend time with her. I came back after

two months. She came back months later. And dumped me…
Humiliation.

During that six-year period I was gambling heavily. I left University because of it. Eventually went to GA and solved my problem… On. My. Own… I never told a soul…

Then my ex-wife… I wasn't perfect. But she made me feel terrible about myself. This marriage breakdown was just the end of the perfect storm that led to the suicide attempt… BUT IT WASN'T HER FAULT AND I NEVER FOR ONE SECOND BLAMED HER.

My therapist asked me how I'd describe women. It was one if those reflex things where you're given no time to think about your responses. My response was: *Cold, dishonest, un-reliable; non-trustworthy.*

The weight shaming and bullying… Years of '*fat bastard*' and '*Alexei Sayle!*' - I also used to get called 'Maradoughnut' (fat Maradona). It hurt and cut deep.

I'd say to anyone who's currently continually taking the piss out of someone, or bullying them, simply think about how they might be feeling.

But I was a twat as well; a piss-taker. Maybe it's Karma? Maybe I got and am getting what I deserved?

All I know is that's a huge part of the reason why I feel worthless. That's why I can't shake the feeling I don't deserve my wife or the children. If I don't manage to get better, she'll leave me. And nobody could argue it wasn't justified.

I told my therapist about what happened at work yesterday. Because I couldn't face standing in the office kitchen for ninety seconds waiting for my soup to heat up… And the prospect of having to talk to people; I went straight to the garden. Sat on my own and ate cold soup out of a can...

She said I'm more unwell that I've let on. It's going to take time to get through this. It is decades of suffering and self-deprecation. No wonder I feel so negative and despondent about myself every single minute of every day.

SATURDAY 23 SEPTEMBER
10.00PM

Pre-holiday planning and discussion – I'm bored of it. But planning is everything on a family trip like this. It's very important to my wife. Probably more-so since we've been together - purely because I'm a dis-organised liability... (I prefer the description 'free spirit'; others prefer 'lazy'.)

- Days since I looked in a mirror? *No idea*
- Days since I took my drops? *No idea*
- Days since I took my inhaler? *No idea*
- Days since I loved or even liked myself... *No idea*

SUNDAY 24 SEPTEMBER
11.50PM

Packing... Well not me... I'll just shove stuff in a bag tomorrow morning.

My mother-in-law paid for the holiday and we're so grateful to her. She's unbelievably kind and generous. This time it's four nights... Draw your own conclusions about how I'll return this time...

Still no funeral or cremation date.

BUTLIN'S

After a decent journey down, we arrived like every other family - enthusiastic and optimistic... Looking forward to our holiday... With excited children full of energy - like coiled springs...

The girls wanted to be everywhere. Our eldest made some friends. (We chatted to the other parents). Bubba looked on intently, grinning from ear to ear. The first night was terrible; the girls couldn't settle. Not what anyone needed – my wife crashed early...

The second day was why we came. Justin Fletcher Live... The kids loved him... Luckily the bar was open. Our eldest burned out and we left before the end. But not before she'd bought her souvenirs. His CD will soon be playing in my house - I want to introduce her to sounds like Bob Marley, The Streets, Orbital, Moby, Roni Size, James Brown, Oasis, Underworld, and Chicane...

The third morning she met her friends at the rides. But the pace was slowing... And the parents - the yawning had started. Shoulders looked more slumped; visibly tired. And patience was starting to wear thin - the telling off, like the cries of the children, getting louder.

The swimming pool was her favourite place. It has huge water slides and a wave machine. Now my eldest is doing well with her swimming lessons. She's so confident - too confident. That evening in the restaurant she barely moved. You could see the batteries draining.

The morning we left she played with her friends. Everywhere I looked there were parents yawning - looking like garbage. Conversations were tetchy; people were marching away from each other. Children were getting pulled along by the wrist; many crying. At the start of the week children were running and parents laughing. Now many, if not most, of the adults looked, and sounded, ready to go home.

I certainly was. But we left with amazing memories. That's all that matters.

Helliday...

Children so happy totally oblivious
Parents are arguing, totally serious

From dawn until dusk, relationships strained
From the looks of some parents, enjoyment so feigned,

Wondering what on earth that they've done,
Thinking 'fuck sake, this certainly ain't fun',

Thankfully every child is full of smiles
To help get them home; all those arduous miles...

SATURDAY 30 SEPTEMBER
8.35PM

Started feeling unwell myself... Bubba has been very bad; a chest like a maraca - but the worst thing has been refusing fluids. And we've had some dry nappies. I was worried. By now you have an idea what I'm like - the irrational fear that something terrible will happen. I've barely been sleeping as it is... This has sent me over the edge.

I can feel a chest infection coming on.

ELEVEN. WORTHLESS HUSBAND; WORTHLESS DADDY, WORTHLESS SON, WORTHLESS GRANDSON

SUNDAY 1 OCTOBER
8.15PM

I was sent upstairs to bed. My wife asked me if I'd showered since we'd got home. My response was a concise *No*. The look she gave me said it all. (That meant about five days) - but when you're unwell these things lose importance. I've been here before. (Maybe you have? Or maybe you're going through this right now? If you are, let me assure you it's a common type of self-neglect.)

But it doesn't make it easier to manage. In fact, it can be worse. Dealing with anger and frustration at myself... *The Why me; why is this happening (again)? Why aren't I stronger?* stuff...

Scolding myself... No way will I be working tomorrow. That makes me paranoid about losing my job. About us losing our home... About losing my wife – it's so scary... I'm losing control.

MONDAY 2 OCTOBER
LATE

Stats from doctor: Chest capacity peak flow 430. Mine should be 660 - 350 means hospital.

I admitted to my doctor I haven't taken medication for a while. For either my mental health or asthma - she wasn't impressed but understood this type of self-neglect is not unusual when people are in my situation. But just asked me to make sure I don't miss any therapy sessions. I nodded; but couldn't make eye contact.

I was signed off for a week. The doctor said I needed rest; and a new; stronger inhaler. That was not what I needed. My paranoia is uncontrollable. It hurts. My chest, my body, my heart...

TUESDAY 3 OCTOBER
MIDNIGHT, OR JUST BEFORE...

I'm feeling down, so disillusioned. I'm taking my asthma medication; but not my head stuff. I suppose I'm half way there. No mirrors though... I just can't face them; literally.

My chest is slightly better, so I've avoided hospital. I must get back to work next week; for so many reasons... It's been at least a week since I got anything like a decent night's sleep. Bubba has been so clingy, barely sleeping, crying most of the time, not eating a lot, and demanding cuddles. Parenting is difficult enough for people who don't have other issues. My problems just exacerbate everything because of my mood swings and hyper-sensitivity. Ah; my old acquaintance, paranoia... I detest you.

WEDNESDAY 4 OCTOBER
10.10PM

I updated my curriculum vitae; which took ages because I was bored and couldn't focus. Within two hours I'd been contacted by three agencies asking about the type of work I'm looking for. Apparently, my C.V. is quite good for someone with no skill set. I said I'm not looking to jump ship immediately, but made it clear my current job will not be long term. It would likely drive me to *The Edge*. And I really don't want to go there again - maybe next time I'll be more, or less successful, depending on which way you look at it...

THURSDAY 5 OCTOBER
10.00PM

Still not looked in the mirror... Worried about Dad; no idea how he's coping – not spoken to him since Nan passed... I'm not feeling anything, as if my insides have been scooped out and dumped in a bin.

FRIDAY 6 OCTOBER
THERAPY

I wasn't thinking about bailing. Just wondering if I'd ever get better... I had a drink beforehand; rum again. I don't know why. Maybe I'll ask my therapist about it. The session next week is three hours before the cremation...

We started with the questionnaire as usual. Some of my scores are lower... But to the question *How often do you think people would be better off with you not around, or alive?* I still answered two - more than half the days.

I said I'm trying to start taking a bit of control of the external things – like updating my CV and registering with recruitment agencies. And that the response had been okay. Although I feel they're only massaging my ego for their own gain... And they don't honestly believe I'm any good. Or have anything to offer.

In terms of the internal things; my therapist talked to me about the concept of acceptance... Maybe this is who I'll always be... And that acceptance will free me from my hang-ups and the negativity.

Was told (again) I need to use mirrors. I replied that most people use them for purely superficial purposes (which I really envy...) But that I can't do that... When I look in a mirror it's like staring into my soul. At all the bad things that have happened to me; all my imperfections - all the things I hate about myself.

I talked about the writing and poetry. That I'm not going to stop doing it despite what my parents might think. Also talked about the fact they don't even really know me - they don't know about the suicide stuff, gambling addiction, or anything really. But I said that I've told some stuff to my wife and that I'll be telling her more soon.

My therapist said it was interesting that I could tell the people helping me with my book implicitly... But struggled with everyone else; including myself. It's simple really – amongst these people - we have some idea of what each other are going through. And most of the times in my life I've made myself vulnerable and trusted people, they've shafted me... So, I don't bother anymore. My therapist said this was very unhealthy. That I needed to forgive myself. And start trying to trust people again. The main crux of the whole thing is that I need to learn how to like and love myself again.

SATURDAY 7 OCTOBER
9.00PM

I was desperate for some family time, but our eldest went to my parents - so I took Bubba for a walk (my wife needed a rest.) She was so good, and now says *hug* too! It's adorable.

Then I thought we'd go for pasta; but little Bubba sparked out.

I had a glass of wine and waited for Mummy to pick us up...

That afternoon we just chilled in the living room - Bubba was calm; my wife relaxing. Getting ready to go out... My God... She looked sensational. I told her if she didn't have her wedding ring on she'd pull. (But maybe the ring wouldn't

make a difference; we all know what some people are like...)
She's a so much better person than me.

SUNDAY 8 OCTOBER
10.00PM

Shocking physical health; shocking mental health... Pains all over; achy joints. Headache, chest pains and acid reflux. Then the paranoia... When will they start building a business case against me? When will I be fired? When will my wife leave me, or kick me out? The house...? How will it be maintained? Will I end up trying something again? Get sectioned? Or will I manage to get better...

MONDAY 9 OCTOBER
HOSPITAL

A night of anxiety, pain, head-tension, insomnia, chest pains and paranoia... The result...? A trip to the hospital... My peak flow was down, chest tight, high temperature and coughing up mucus – the usual.

After four hours of blood tests, x-rays, scans and an ECG the outcome was a diagnosed chest infection, and another inflammatory respiratory condition. Ten pills a day (eight steroids) for the next five days. I've not taken my drops for two days.

TUESDAY 10 OCTOBER
11.50PM

The steroids are nasty… Ever taken them? Then you'll know what I mean. Forty milligrams of the stuff a day is excessive. They are helping my chest; but the side effects are bad.

A few hours of crazy energy, unable to sit still or focus on anything, and then… The sweats, the shakes, a fever, freezing cold – wrapped up in a blanket, sweating, freezing, shaking, drifting in and out of consciousness… Lasting about three hours…

Then the grotty come down; if you've ever taken speed…

WEDNESDAY 11 OCTOBER
PAST MIDNIGHT

The steroids have stopped me from working and being a parent and a husband for three days.

If the girls start sleeping through the night anytime soon that would be a fantastic, beautiful, thing. And if I can start sorting my body clock out and sleeping at a reasonable hour too…

I really don't want much.

No two households are the same. I bet yours is totally different to your mates'. But it's about getting to a place which is right for you… And I think slowly, it feels like we're getting there…

I looked in a mirror after months of avoidance… It was hard…

I saw a man who should be in the prime of his life, looking old. Grey receding hair, big bags under the eyes; greying chest hair and a fat stomach… A man in nowhere near peak physical condition; or even attractive…

It's hard to say, but honest…

I saw the eyes of a man who has lost his way, his direction and his zest for life. Of someone who is tired, physically and mentally, wasted potential and broken promises to his wife and children. But looking deeper, the eyes of a man who hasn't given up. Who is coming to terms with his mental issues, trying to resolve them, and be a good husband and dad.

The other thing I did was make a list of good and bad things about me… I made this decision myself, to try and dig deeper… You reckon this is easy? I tell you, it is not. Go on – try it. You might even find out something about yourself…

Bad: Unattractive, unfit, overweight and sweaty – any looks I had have faded. Selfish, self-centred, severely mentally unbalanced, temperamental and moody… Unpredictable and unable to deal with plans and constraints; occasional binge-drinking… A bad listener and borderline ignorant (some of the time…) - and need a lot of me time… A failed education and unfinished degree… A rubbish friend and broke…

Good: Loving, sensitive and caring. I try my best; I want to be a good father, husband, brother, son and friend. Honest and

I have integrity. I want to better myself. I have family values, I try to be a good role model and do the best I can for my wife and children. I'm conscientious and empathetic. I'm ambitious and never give up. I want to make people happy. Writing, I think. Travel and life experience, I think.

I'm going to take all this to therapy tomorrow… Glad it's before Nan's cremation.

FRIDAY 13 OCTOBER
11.00PM

Struggling to think straight - or write. Burps and hiccups are pure acid and boozy barf - but I'm still drinking.

The cremation… Was…. I'll just settle for 'horrible'… I knew I wouldn't cry. Dry as a bone. At the wake I sat on my own. Sipping rum… Letting everything go on around me…

The girls were beautiful distractions… Everyone was besotted by them.

No food for me…

As the rum haze descended - I spoke to a few of my family.

My uncle asked me about the poem. He'd heard I'd been thinking of reading. That was it - the service. It was impersonal… It didn't reflect Nan's amazing life. I said I'd send him the poem tomorrow.

At about seven o'clock I asked my wife to take the girls home. As people started to leave the drinking became harder; quicker.

The pain was increasing and decreasing at the same time.

Increasing as the grief and finality set in - no more grandparents left… But decreasing as the blood alcohol level increased.

(Just dropped my phone - fell over as I tried to go for a piss. Booted my drink everywhere…)

Eventually it was just my parents, me and my dear cousin - shots and shooters followed. As well as a few tears.

In between sips we talked about old times; our family and friends; good and bad - reminiscing; that's what it's about right? Drinking…? It just happens.

At mine? I'll be making sure only the finest rum and lager is served. I'll choose somewhere that I'll hopefully have spent years having weekend lunches with my daughters.

The food…? Jerk chicken; spicy… The finest steak… Plantain, rice… Snapper and king prawn with citrus cheesecake. Rum and raisin ice cream. And reggae music.

I feel so sorry for my dad. I want to help him; to make things better - easier. But I'm powerless.

I've nothing left.

SATURDAY 14 OCTOBER
CARNIVAL DISTRACTION

By some miracle I felt okay first thing.

So, a big day… Lunch with my brother-in-law was nice. When we reached the fair, he gave our eldest two bags full of coins. So, I bought lunch.

My eldest and I went on rides together for the first time. I think I enjoyed it more than she did…

But;

How can two consecutive days be so different? How can it be right? How can it be fair?

Being happy doesn't feel right.

Life sucks.

SUNDAY 15 OCTOBER
8.45PM

My mental health has dramatically improved. The reasons why? I'm trying not to be the victim anymore. I'm trying to realise that I'm not useless. And I just haven't found my vocation in life - but there's still time. Time for all of us...

Yes, I'm trapped in my job due to financial commitments. But it won't always be this way. And I'll soon have alternatives. You do too, if you want them or really look. But for the time being I just want; and need to be a provider. My job is secure and I'm grateful. But that's not who I am or what I'll be remembered for. No way.

MONDAY 16 OCTOBER
10.33PM

Starting to feel a bit down… Not about having to go back to work. Just that my job isn't for me anymore. Surely thousands of people have or are experiencing these feelings every day... Maybe you are?

I decided to go to the lake for a few hours just to clear my head. Sometimes we can change the way we feel. And when we can, we must at least try.

Look – it is all very well people telling you this. But it means nothing. What's important is that you as a person can recognise this, and do something about it - for me? It's taken twelve sessions of therapy spanning sixteen months. And although I feel a bit better right now I'm not fixed. It's a day-to-day thing.

All this might sound boring and dull. But if you're living with someone with a mental illness, this is some of what they might be feeling.

Six weeks ago, from the outside I looked and sounded fine; but leaving the house was so painful. I felt scared and a failure. It was embarrassing. But once I admitted I was struggling again I could start to get help. But again; if you're living with someone like me - you can only do so much. You can't get them help. They need to be ready to want and accept help. But just being there for us is more than we could ever ask. Thank you for loving us, supporting us, and standing by us x

TUESDAY 17 OCTOBER
10.00PM

Feeling a bit better… Even a colleague said I looked well. Honestly? I don't remember the last time someone said that to me. I was so stunned I didn't know what to say. I just mumbled a load of uncomfortable gibberish. It's a life lesson - just one tiny thing; a small compliment - but it means so much to someone.

It put me on an upward curve; kept the momentum going.

I try to complement my wife and children as much as I can - and my parents when I see them. Or I'll sometimes just send Mum a quick text. It makes me feel good just knowing how hearing or reading them makes other people feel.

Our eldest seems happy. It's no coincidence. I'm happy - and she feels it. Her language skills are coming along great. Some of the things she says are amazing *Daddy, this lemon is sharp* or *Daddy, have a good day; hope you earn lots of pennies*. I'm so proud of her and tell her every day. We'll soon be looking at primary schools. If you've been through this, you know how I'm feeling! A decision that's going to have a huge impact on your child's life... It's a privilege, but a huge responsibility.

My wife has turned into mummy cub - the loneliness protecting her cubbies. I love her so much. She'll make sure we make the right decision. I've offered my opinion from time to time. But this must be right for her, that's all that matters.

WEDNESDAY 18 OCTOBER
9.00PM

It's been a good day. I slept better and am talking to people more. Not working as hard as I was but I'm starting to show people glimpses of my real personality. The person who is hidden from the rest of the world most of the time.

For a week I've been self-medicating; properly. Taking both inhaler and drops twice a day... And I'm using mirrors. I'm feeling physically better than I have for months.

The house is calmer; we're all tired, but happy. With anything, but especially mental illness; you must be right, before you can help and support others. Maybe it's finally sinking in? Maybe I'm starting to reconnect with my old self? Even starting to love myself again? I'm always tentative about progress. We all are, aren't we? We try not to get carried away? But for now, the signs are good... For us, but also our partners, it's a day by day thing. We sometimes forget what our partners live through because we are so consumed by our illness. But we should never forget.

THURSDAY 19 OCTOBER
10.55PM

Pleased it's the end of the week. I need some time with the girls...

My asthma appointment was pointless; same old routine. Take your inhaler; take one during the day if you need it - blah blah. I admitted my mental health was bad – and I wasn't taking my inhaler, I had to be honest. I need to book another appointment...

FRIDAY 20 OCTOBER
ABOUT 10.30PM

Well that was different! The labouring (sweeping floors and knocking up plaster) was just around the corner from my ex-parents-in-law... I didn't like it. We went to the shop. I kept thinking one of her family was going to walk around the corner and see me. Horrible paranoia; surprised I wasn't sick on the floor... I could barely eat. Lucky we were stuck in a loft conversion all day... Like a metaphor for my mental state – Enclosed, dark and empty.

SATURDAY 21 OCTOBER
8.52PM

We played board games all day – our eldest still cheats! Then scooting, she's fast. But still doesn't look where she's going (just like me). It was great. Bubba is everywhere. Reaching, grabbing and pulling... Nothing is safe anymore! They're both so pretty.

The evening was okay. Nice to be out but didn't get to talk much. The one time I was ready and felt comfortable enough to do it. After a lot of build-up in my head and tension; I kind of slipped back into my shell. The lager flowed freely... And I was invited to France for a weekend fishing trip. I got home and carried on drinking. I can barely see. I'm holding my phone in two hands; typing with two hands - the screen right up against my face. And this is still taking me ages...

SUNDAY 22 OCTOBER
MIDNIGHT

I felt terrible this morning. I woke up on the floor at half past five.

Mum and Dad came which was a blessing. They entertained the girls, so we tried to do the housework. I fell asleep on the small sofa in the afternoon.

I should have been helping. This is nothing to do with my mental health. It's just woeful behaviour. It was out of order, right? I'm sure many of you are nodding. But then how many people are brave enough to admit their failings and disgraceful behaviour? Less than you think, for sure.

I'll never use mental health as an excuse for that. I've told my wife this.

We talked about France. I don't think she's happy.

Text to my wife…

You don't ever have to apologise. You've stuck by me over the last year. When my mental illness has been bad… Some people have walked away; or just brushed my problems under the carpet. And I know I've been horrible to be around at times. That's not acceptable for you. You deserve a much better quality of life; when you do so much for us all. I'm feeling much better now. I'm self-medicating every day. And I'm trying to be more responsible and less selfish. Last night was a blow out and not ideal behaviour. But I'm trying my best every day. To make you as happy as you make me. I know my mental illness is sometimes bad. But I will never use that as an excuse for piss poor behaviour. And I love that you blow a gasket every now and again. You're one of the few people in my life who is totally honest with me. And that's why I love and respect you. Even though I know you could do so much better than me. (I've talked to my therapist about this; and my very close friends. It might be irrational. But it's also a fair comment. But that's not your prob-lem. It's mine). I know I'm a twat. But I'm honestly trying every day to be a better man. And I won't stop trying. I'm also going to be more honest with you; about my past and illness. But there's so much. So, it must be in small doses. But you can always ask me anything. Anytime... xx

MONDAY 23 OCTOBER
9.00PM

My first full day back at work was okay. No paranoia. No self-loathing; still working on self-worth. But it'll take a while and I'm comfortable with that. I'm enjoying talking to people. It's been ages since I last felt like that.

My wife is poorly again - she must be so run down. She's been bad on and off for a couple of months. I honestly don't think I'll ever feel I do enough for her; or be enough for her.

We've had a few bad nights because Bubba's teeth are coming down. She's coping so well though and chomping all sorts! We're back to hugs, Calpol and broken sleep. The weird thing...? I'm going to miss this so much. Soon neither of the girls will need me for anything... They'll get everything else from their mum - shopping trips, fashion advice and emotional support.

I'll just be the engine running in the background. Working, sleeping and working.

Breaking the mould…

Breaking Bad…

My first fifteen-minute lunchtime run at work… (And the first episode of my only box set attempt since The Sopranos… The ending, the ending!)

Didn't tell anyone at work until someone clocked me… I hated that moment.

I've also now got a new swimming chum. So now the challenge is to keep the exercise up. At work I'm breaking the mould - breaking my mould. And trying to take some control back… And it feels good.

I'm not a lover of box-sets; or television generally. I prefer documentaries. But I'm going to finish Breaking Bad. You've probably seen it.

I'm miles behind popular culture; particularly social media, which can be vile. But for people like me, like you, like us, like someone we know, social media not only worsens existing mental illness, it can create it. But it can also do amazing things. I'd just say to anyone, use it carefully. You only need to look at the news to see cases of suicide following online bullying. It makes my heart break.

I'm already thinking about when I'll have to start talking to the girls about it. I'm sure many of you are battling the same fears… And it's the thought of losing control of your children, not being able to always be there to protect them too, right?

It'll be the same with their boyfriends too. They will be put through the ringer. I'm sure the girls will fall out with me. I'm not looking forward to it... The problem is I'll only love them more as every day passes. And I'll be even more protective. Looking into your future can be amazing... But terrifying too can't it...?

WEDNESDAY 25 OCTOBER
10.10PM

France trip – check!

Free childcare renewal - check!

Wait… Aaarrggggggggghhhhhhhhhh! Got home, my ladies were kicking off and strung out - don't blame my wife. Two children can push anyone to the limit, can't they? I jumped in to help. It was manic. Then she asked me to do the free child-care renewal after the girls were down. I rushed to get it done. You know what it's like? When you think the gasket is going to blow. Well, I messed the form up; came down from story time and just snapped. The gasket ended up somewhere down the road. It happens. But you feel sick in the pit of your stomach when it does right? Wish you'd thought before opening your fat mouth? It's tough... Apology and humble pie time... My head felt like it was being clamped. My mental health is just about okay. I reassured my wife of that. I tried to be honest.

If I'd been in a dark place I wouldn't have slept a wink last night; replaying everything over in my head from my little blow up.

The day flew - scary... I wonder if when you're on your death bed it's the same. Everything's relative, though I hope it is - a few seconds flashing through the seminal moments of your life; sending you off with fond memories. Maybe that's the pay off? Maybe I'm a romantic? No, I'm definitely, a romantic. Maybe I'm talking rubbish? No, I'm definitely talking rubbish. Doesn't mean you shouldn't though. Doesn't make it wrong either...

Talking about death isn't wrong either. It shouldn't be taboo; it's healthy. So is planning. What's the point in not planning for the inevitable? In many cultures a funeral or cremation is a real festival, a proper celebration of life. That's how it should be. There won't be any black when I'm lowered into the ground or toasted.

FRIDAY 27 OCTOBER

SO FAR PAST MIDNIGHT IT'S ALMOST LIGHT

Party preparations - trick or treating next week, and Nanny's Halloween party. At times of mega excitement; as parents there's only one thing you can do... Let them run around in a wide-open space! Today, the wildlife park came to our rescue. Our eldest struts around like she owns it. Knows where everything is; knows what she wants. Bubba is now enjoying it much more. She was watching the animals jump around. And doing proper belly laughs - it was so cute!

My addictive personality has resurfaced. 'Breaking Bad' is now an unhealthy obsession. I've done two series in four nights. That means running on about three hours sleep a night. It's now nearly three o'clock.

My younger sister is pregnant. Mum told me. But I'm not supposed to know so I've not contacted her. I hope she's okay and things go smoothly. I'll talk to her soon... So happy for her.

SATURDAY 28 OCTOBER
EVEN LATER THAN LAST NIGHT

The house was a dump this morning, so I took the girls for breakfast. (Walked the double buggy I mean.) It's hard work but always nice to be out with them.

Bubba's teething again so days and nights are hard; but so much harder for her. Love you, Bubba x

Nanny's Halloween party was supposed to be a welcome distraction...

Our eldest was manic; so over-excited. At one point she caught her head badly on a door handle - just not paying attention. But she's like me. I'll never change. I don't want her to either.

But it was two hours of dancing with Daddy, sugary food and running; fun but exhausting. Our relationship is so much better than three months ago. Yes, it's partly because my mental health is better. But that's because I've been working at it - remember? I never used it as excuse. When I wasn't self-medicating? Yes, I was unwell. But it was still my responsibility; my choice. And I decided to punish myself, to not allow myself to start feeling better.

With the children sleeping it's darts, France preparation and wine for me.

And a quiet, peaceful and happy house...

Magic.

SUNDAY 29 OCTOBER
8.00PM

So busy today... Very little sleep last night. Not too much family stuff. The van is loaded for France. It should be a great trip - my first European fishing adventure. I'm going to miss my three beautiful ladies. Hopefully alcohol, exhaustion, sleep and relaxation will quell that fire...

MONDAY 30 OCTOBER
10.03PM

My therapist and I concluded the France trip will be better for me than my last session. This set has been much harder and more challenging than the first time. But I was very unwell a few months ago. It was very worrying - that the thoughts about self-harm and suicide were so strong. Yet I felt so calm about the possible outcome. If you feel like that ever, then I urge you to talk to someone - immediately. It has saved my life; at least once. It could save yours, or the life of someone you love... I honestly and sincerely believe this; from the bottom of my heart.

So, after seven weeks of therapy what have I realised?

- I'm not perfect; I never will be. But I'm becoming comfortable with that - acceptance
- I deserve to have a wife and children who love me
- I must stop setting myself impossible standards. They're pointless and very damaging
- I have not wasted my life
- I have time to achieve the rest of my goals
- I'm lucky to be in my situation, to have what I have. And must try to never forget that
- Suicide doesn't solve anything
- I'm talented
- Being selfish can be good
- Pleasing other people all the time is not healthy
- I'm a good father
- It's acceptable not to cry at funerals. It doesn't mean you're not sad; or dead inside. Emotional expression comes in many forms
- It's okay to accept praise when I do good things
- It's okay to need, ask for, and accept help

- It's okay to be vulnerable; we all are in our own way
- I'm important; I matter
- It's okay to be wrong, and to admit mistakes
- Self-medication is critical to well-being. Not self-medicating is a form of self-harm
- I need to stop punishing myself
- I should trust my judgements
- I need to love myself.

I think that although I may never be right... Currently I'm doing okay. I'm more comfortable, at peace, and happy.

Here's my therapy exit questionnaire...

Over the last two weeks, how often have you been bothered by any of the following problems?

SCORING SCALE – 0: Not at all, 1: Several days, 2: More than half the days, 3: Nearly every day

- Little or no interest in doing things: 0
- Feeling down, depressed or hopeless: 1
- Trouble falling/staying asleep: 1
- Feeling tired or having little energy: 1
- Poor appetite or overeating: 1
- Feeling bad about yourself - or that you're a failure or have let yourself or your family down: 2
- Trouble concentrating on things, such as reading the newspaper or watching television: 1
- Moving or speaking so slowly that other people could have

noticed. Or the opposite – being so fidgety or restless that you have been moving around a lot more than usual: 1

- Thoughts that you would be better off dead or of hurting yourself in some way: 1

SCORE: 9/27

Over the last two weeks, how often have you been bothered by any of the following problems?

SCORING SCALE – 0: Not at all, 1: Several days, 2: More than half the days, 3: Nearly every day

- Feeling nervous, anxious or on edge: 1
- Not being able to stop or control worrying: 1
- Worry too much about different things: 1
- Trouble relaxing: 1
- Being so restless that it is hard to sit still: 1
- Becoming easily annoyed or irritable: 1
- Feeling afraid as if something awful might happen: 1

SCORE: 7/21

Choose a number from the scale below to show how much you would avoid each of the situations or objects listed below.

SLIDING SCALE: 0: Never Avoid it, 4: Slightly avoid it, 8: Always avoid it.

- Social situations due to fear of being embarrassed or making a fool of myself: 1

- Certain situations because of a fear of having a panic attack or other distressing symptoms (such as loss of bladder control, vomiting or dizziness): 0
- Certain situations because of a fear of particular objects or activities (such as animals, heights, seeing blood, being in confined spaces, driving or flying): 3

SCORE: 4/24

People's problems sometimes affect their ability to do certain day-to-day tasks in their lives. To rate your problems, look at each section below and determine on the scale provided, how much your problem impairs your ability to carry out the activity

SLIDING SCALE: 0: Not at all, 4: Definitely, 8: Very severely/I cannot work.

- Work: 2
- Home management: 1
- Social leisure activities: 1
- Private leisure activities: 0
- Family and relationships: 2

SCORE: 6/40

Halloween...

Our eldest was ready to go. A witch on the move! She's so lucky; our cul-de-sac is full of nice people; and the children have so much fun. Even Bubba got a little chocolate ghost, ate it, and immediately wanted more! Its days like this that makes you realise what a total privilege raising a family is. Sometimes I cry a little at the end of evenings like this.

I'm working hard on my mental health. The self-medication is becoming a bigger part of my routine - I'm sleeping better – the last ten days or so I've been sleeping upstairs. Now sleep is only broken if one of the girls wakes up.

I had no idea how this was going to pan out when I started writing ten months ago. I certainly wasn't expecting to self-refer, back into therapy. But that's the beauty of this. I don't know what's going to happen. Neither do you. It's real. But I hope you're getting something from this. Be it a shared experience, advice, a moment of realisation, or simply some comfort in the fact you're not alone. And that it's okay for everyone, especially men, to talk about how they feel.

TWELVE. BROKEN

Self-medication is still going well. Daily discipline is a daily battle; but paying off. It's exactly how I felt during my battle with gambling. The first few weeks after the GA sessions ended; when you're raw and so vulnerable. There's temptation everywhere, and you have to avoid situations where you can gamble.

And it's the shame too... I felt so ashamed of what I'd done to myself, and how my addiction, and how my lying and deception, had affected the lives of people around me.

But that was my motivation to get better. Of course, it was for me, but just as much for the people around me. So, they didn't have to put up with my illness any more.

Every minute is a battle. But every one that passes makes you stronger; more resilient. Ever been through addiction? If so, I totally get it. It's horrible. You become a zombie, a slave to it. But I hope you've found help. And come out of the other side. We can win. We will win.

GA was one of the most amazing experiences of my life. I would recommend it to anyone.

If you think you might need some help along these lines you

could start by going to the Gamblers Anonymous website, here you can find out about what GA does and where the nearest meeting to you is.

But now it's Breaking Bad and wine… My holiday has started…

THURSDAY 2 NOVEMBER
9.39PM

Too much wine last night… The girls had bad nights; I was a state; and had Bubba downstairs until about four o'clock… Then our eldest was up just after five. I chained cups of coffee for about three hours but was hanging when I was picked up.

The drive was long; six hours front door to lake… Which was tiny, shallow and full of weed. We arrived an hour before dusk. The owners are lovely. As is their hospitality and food.

Had a few beers and ready to crash out - the fact the lake is not what we expected is annoying. Especially considering how far we've travelled.

FRIDAY 3 NOVEMBER
10.30PM

It's a lovely place - relaxing and therapeutic. Good for the soul. France is a beautiful country; such a lovely place to live. I love the people too. I'd happily retire here. Not so sure about my wife…

I left my medication at home. I'm feeling okay but don't want to slip. I've worked so hard to get where I am...

It's nice being here with two of my good fishing buddies - lovely blokes who will change the world in the next few years - I'm seriously impressed and proud of them.

Been quaffing port since lunchtime... Caught two small fish and stuffed my face. I'm feeling at peace. Desperately trying to savour and appreciate it. I've been so unwell. I just want to enjoy every minute of this.

But there's always something to bring you back to reality. In my life anyway... Here? I got my times wrong. *We're back tomorrow night. Not tomorrow morning.* I can't babysit while my wife and our eldest go to the fireworks display – I'm in the bad books; my life is never simple.

I had to organise an alternative to prevent getting into more trouble. Luckily my parents came to my rescue. I'd have been screwed otherwise.

SATURDAY 4 NOVEMBER
MIDDAY

I'm currently in the back of the van. I woke up and it was raining. Ate breakfast in the rain; packed up in the rain. And we drove away in the rain...

I'm missing the girls so much; all three of them. I don't know what I'd do if they weren't in my life... Well I do... but that's nobody else's problem.

It's the longest I've ever been away from everyone. And the

first time I've gone abroad without them. Bedtimes were weird this trip; relaxed, but ever so empty...

Got to do my therapy exit questionnaires this weekend - it'll be interesting to compare them to when I started two months ago. Once completed, I'll share them with you, so you'll have basically gone through the whole therapy experience with me.

I hope it's been useful. It might answer some questions and banish misconceptions. It might help some people decide that therapy is for them. Maybe even for you... If it even helps one person that would be enough.

10.30PM

Sofa...? Check... Breaking Bad? Check... Port...? Check...! That was a rancid journey home though... And I'm rancid - you know it's bad when you can smell yourself right? I really should be having a shower.

Tomorrow will be full on... I can't wait to see everyone. Missing family is horrible isn't it? But a massive thing is not feeling guilty when I'm away. That's huge. Believing I deserve a short break.

SUNDAY 5 NOVEMBER
8.20PM

What a lovely day. The girls are amazing. Seems like Bubba has grown a headful of hair in three days! She looks so much like me it's scary. She now does 'high fives' and makes cooing noises to her favourite song!

Our eldest is now bossy and articulate. Can't believe how tall and beautiful she is - she amazes me every day. If I live until I'm eighty-five. I'll be around for the first forty-five years of their lives. And see in our 50th wedding anniversary.

That would be nice...

MONDAY 6 NOVEMBER
9.00PM

Back to the monotony of work - headset stuck to my head; in the 'I don't care' min-dset...

It feels good to be back on my medication after two days off.

Bus was late; then broke down. Then my train was late. Bravo world... Trying to break me... Seeing if I'll cave... My karma, my soul, tells me this is payback for going away; leaving my wife with the girls. The difference here is that the guilt feels right, not irrational.

TUESDAY 7 NOVEMBER
9.54PM

Work is dull; same repeated sequence.

Had the mental health app idea today, and the idea for a mental health support and engagement programme for professional sport. It's very early days. But I want to give it everything.

I'm not going to die wondering... If you have a dream, idea or plan; whatever it is. Seize the day. Don't worry; don't fret. Crack on. Our ideas are worth it. So are we.

Our eldest is swimming unaided! It's sad I never see her lessons but there's nothing I can do. In the morning before I go to work, she says, *I love you, dada, hope you earn some pennies.* I'm smiling as I'm writing.

WEDNESDAY 8 NOVEMBER
9.00PM

Last night was horrendous... When you're used to a baby sleeping through the night, then there are wake-ups, it's brutal. You could rest satsumas in the bags under my eyes.

Been called for a blood test Friday - reckon it's related to the one I had on my liver last year. But I'll have to do what the doctors say. And be honest about my drinking. *It's still bingey...*

Not bought any Christmas presents yet... If it wasn't for my wife we'd be totally stuffed... She's amazing. Every day she shows me - without even trying.

THURSDAY 9 NOVEMBER
11.00PM

Panic - I've got very little money; big birthdays coming up and Christmas presents to buy... The self-loathing is creeping back; as well as the failure complex... It's consuming me

– hating myself.

I need to go to bed… Once my mind has stopped racing… But there feels no sign of slowing. I'm going to be up for a while - laying here in the dark. My heart is pumping and sweat-beads rolling down my face.

FRIDAY 10 NOVEMBER
8.00PM

Blood test went badly - couldn't get any blood out of my left arm, from a vein they've never used before. Tried the right arm; immediate success. I left the doctor with pins and needles all the way down my left arm. They told me to stay so they could monitor me. I walked out anyway; my arm tingling and bleeding.

I'm doing a lot of writing for the website and app. I'm proud of what I'm doing and that I'm trying to do something to help people. Even if it never comes off, I can say I've tried my best (I'll still feel a failure). Nice drop of port now. It's been a long week; and well deserved.

SATURDAY 11 NOVEMBER
9.00PM

Bubba had a terrible night. She woke up hysterical. I cuddled her for ages after her medicine; and she slowly calmed down. It's heart-breaking watching one of your children cry. Especially when they're normally so happy... We'd all take that pain for our children if we could...

I woke up steaming. Met my sister for a catch up... And told her about the gambling and suicide stuff. She was shocked. She told me her news. I acted surprised.

At least I went home sober; and able to contribute... Feeling the pace now.

SUNDAY 12 NOVEMBER
8.30PM

Hectic...

Cleaned for four hours - short rest - parents for dinner; total chaos. Crap everywhere. Everyone was tearing around. I was letting things pass me by - happy not being the centre of attention. Writing is becoming a huge part of my life. And yeah; I'm not doing it for the money. It's not everything is it? I'm just trying to do something good.

If you're doing the same, be proud of yourself - so often low paid jobs are the most emotionally and spiritually rewarding. I've done support and volunteer work in the past. It's better to have a full heart than full pockets.

A room with a view (into your mind)

A room so small, so private, but enables
Two people, to create a place so stable,
You can open your heart, share your fears
Not worry about shedding all those tears,

That's a sign of the pain that holds you back
But by sharing all this, you're on the right track,
To realising that this is not all your fault
That your open wounds don't need any salt,

Therapy takes time, but time helps to heal
Those wounds which will hopefully help you feel,
So much better, so when you look in the mirror
The person looking back has more than a glimmer,

Of the person you were before all this started
And the person you are now the last session has ended

It's about eleven months since I started this. I'll probably end on New Year's Eve. It feels right.

I'll be able to end with some proper reflection. (Any) lessons learned, cautionary tales and hopes for next year. For myself; my beautiful wife and children. For parents, people suffering with mental illness. For you... You're the most important part of all this. I'm doing this so hopefully you can help yourself or someone close to you.

This is the best I've felt for a while. I feel close to my wife and feel like things are better than they've been for some time. But she hasn't had to put up with as much of my illness and bad behaviour because I've been improving.

At home I'm *Good daddy.* Our eldest tells me she loves me every day. And this week even asked me to do her bed time story.

A few months ago, I didn't think my year, or the book, would end well. Because life doesn't always work out the way we want it to, does it? But if this is two things, it's honest and real.

I hope it's showing that you never truly know what's going on in someone's head. *You'll only ever know what people want you to know...* Nobody even started to know me until a few months ago. Not even those closest to me. The only way that happened was by breaking the silence and the barriers... And (take a deep breath, Alpha Males), by opening-up.

TUESDAY 14 NOVEMBER
9.50PM

A couple of bad nights on the trot - teething is the worst part of parenting in the early years; even worse than the first injections - because that pain is gone in minutes. Working full time on broken sleep is rough. But we're getting through it together - that's how we'll win.

I'm feeling like a better father and husband. My self-worth and self-esteem, which is ludicrously fragile, is slowly growing.

Writing is giving me a new dimension. I'm doing everything I told myself and my therapist I'd do; for now. But it shows what we can do and the potential we have. Nothing is ever easy. But it's important to keep goals, hopes, dreams and desires at the forefront of our minds. That's what keeps the fire burning.

WEDNESDAY 15 NOVEMBER
9.00PM

Call from my therapist. I've got to go back for my final session.

Letter from the doctor. Need to contact them about my blood test results...

THURSDAY 16 NOVEMBER.
THERAPY EXIT FEEDBACK FORM

My therapist was excellent - professional; empathetic; honest; kind; genuine and sincere. The referral and initial assessment were efficient - quick first and subsequent appointments.

My therapist always listened to me, never once interrupting. She gave me time and space. She asked me difficult questions and challenged me. She was always honest and helped me process my thinking and motivations.

She listened and helped me to start to find the root causes of my problems and helped me process them.

My therapist kept me focused so we could identify my barriers and progress.

She discussed ideas on my level, which enabled me to use the sessions as I wanted. At the pace I wanted and needed... I was given the tools I needed to help myself. It was the combination of all these things that enabled me to slowly start my healing process.

I'm truly grateful to my therapist for everything she has done for me...

If this ever gets published, you know who you are... Thank you sincerely...

FRIDAY 17 NOVEMBER
10.42PM

Still feeling emotional after the session yesterday... Luckily, I'm not working today.

Our eldest was up at four o'clock. *Dada, I'm not tired* so I plonked her on the sofa with warm blackcurrant. She was fine. Me? Yup; wide awake - so I cleaned; going back and forth to the bins. The neighbours must've been furious. I suppose I'll find out in a few hours. By which time I'll still not have had any sleep and won't be sociable or have any patience whatsoever.

Bubba's teething has triggered my insomnia. My sleep pattern is gone. Even for someone who's used to functioning on very little sleep it's been tough.

SATURDAY 18 NOVEMBER
11.00PM

For once we sat down, and all ate together. It was lovely. We've promised we'll try and do it more often. We shared food and laughs. I loved it.

The red wine tastes good. I'm going to have a headache.

SUNDAY 19 NOVEMBER
9.50PM

Massive headache - can't sit in one position for too long. Can't get comfortable; can't relax. Just took some pills. Hoping they'll work.

Spoke to my dad this afternoon. He'd been at my nan's house sorting things out... He sounded a bit better.

MONDAY 20 NOVEMBER
6.10PM

A 'Grade A' pants day at work. I feel like I'm just wasting away - if I'm healthy I'll probably work another thirty years. That's not long to make a difference. It seems like ages doesn't it? But it's nothing. Life is short; my clock is ticking. Time is precious. That's why I work so much outside work. And spend as much time as I can with my family.

Had a text from my wife – our eldest has just woken from a cat-nap. It's six o'clock. She'll be up for hours. Not getting the rub off the green lately but it's a familiar feeling. The train has pulled in - time for some air. Need to get rid of all the crazy, manic darkness in my head.

Christmas is supposed to be a time of joy isn't it? Stress, church (for some) presents and crap telly. But it is also a time of year relationships break down; domestic abuse spikes, people self-harm and take their lives. They get into debt and max-out credit cards. I get it... How is the everyday man in the street supposed to be able to afford everything? Spend within your means? Absolutely - start buying presents early? Just what we did... But when you only have one income to support the whole house it's very hard. It's so stressful. It's easy to understand how money causes so much stress and so many problems.

In Kenya a person went into a church, detonated an explosive and killed fifty innocent people. In the year I've been writing the book, there have been eight major terror attacks/mass murders - in Berlin, Manchester, London, Barcelona, Finland, New York, Las Vegas and Kenya – At least 190 people have lost their lives. It's just so sad.

Perspective is so important. My medication is crucial. I haven't looked in a mirror for a week. I can't bear the thought of what might look back at me. It makes my skin crawl - like I just want to peel it off, layer after layer.

WEDNESDAY 22 NOVEMBER
5.00PM

So last October I had blood tests for a general health MOT. I explained that prior to therapy I was drinking hard - for about four months caning spirits like water. Then I had a liver function test. I recorded 220; the average being seventy. Four weeks ago, I had a yearly check-up. I was expecting it to be worse. (Even though I've knocked spirits on the head, have been exercising and drinking plenty of water). To my surprise, my liver function was 140. The doctor said she was happier but not totally happy. She's asked me to have a non-urgent liver and stomach ultrasound. To be honest it's good; I need to know where I am.

Days of diary left? Thirty-nine.

9.00PM

The girls had a late nap and wouldn't go down. The freezer is broken, there's ice everywhere. I'd not stopped since five this morning. The toys were lobbed out of my adult pram. I lost it. I'm still manic. Head's all over the place. In this state I shouldn't be around anyone. I just sent my wife a text saying exactly that. I'll be crashing on the sofa tonight.

Best place for me.

THURSDAY 23 NOVEMBER
1.30PM

Two hundred pounds switch money from Nationwide tomorrow gets us out of a tight spot. It's lifted my mood slightly... I hate that money can affect me so much. And can affect us all.

Don't remember the last time I felt so flat at work. Just got to try and grit my teeth until Christmas.

FRIDAY 24 NOVEMBER
10.00PM

Personalised Christmas presents are driving me insane. They take hours. And websites have been crashing due to heavy traffic. I nearly bunted my laptop out the window.

Our eldest still has a bruised eye from when a boy jabbed her with a fork at nursery. Lucky, I didn't see him do it. I'd have picked him up by both ankles and slung him in a wheelie bin. Don't like it? Shocked? You don't have to agree. Don't care if you judge. Although a calm person generally I have rage. It's always the quiet ones, right? I could feel it simmering. That's why I removed myself from that situation.

Self-medication's still going well. Not using mirrors. No idea why... No scan date yet... I need to lay off the booze though.

But I enjoy it. That's why I haven't. It's the selfish side of me again. Why am I not making decisions based on what's right for everyone? I know what my therapist would say.. It's just another form of self-harm - punishing myself without people seeing or knowing.

SATURDAY 25 NOVEMBER
8.00PM

This afternoon we went to the Christmas lights' turn on in the town square. It was freezing. But the atmosphere - generated by the crowd - was warm. Not everyone is lucky enough to enjoy family time like this. I held Bubba for about half an hour. She was mesmerised; eyes wide and bulging - trying to take everything in.

I wish my nan was still around. I miss her every day. It's going to be a weird Christmas for me and Dad - his first with no parents; my first with no grandparents. I hope he manages okay. I love him like a brother. He's so much more than a dad.

SUNDAY 26 NOVEMBER
7.39PM

I'm in bed. I'm tired. And my body aches. It's not nice.

When days are full on they can just get on top of you can't they? I love how much energy the girls have. And their love for life; I just wish some of it would rub off on me. Ever feel like you're being left behind? It feels like I'm slowing. But everything else is getting quicker...

Sunday night - if you're in a functional job you're already dreaming of Friday. I know I am. I'm living for the weekends.

MONDAY 27 NOVEMBER
10.15PM

Bought the last of the Christmas presents... I'm tired. I've got the raging hump, but I'm done. I'm sick of laptops and websites.

I can hear Bubba crying. I pulled some of my hair out; could be a long night. My temper is frayed and short. Simmering...

TUESDAY 28 NOVEMBER
8.58PM

Yeah; last night was bad. I spent more time on the stairs than anywhere else. Head in hands - slumped; hunched over my knees. Times like this you're reminded just how vulnerable babies and little children are. How they're totally reliant on you. And you control their every experience - shape their lives. When you're at your wit's end and totally lost your patience. It's easy to lose sight of that.

I can feel the temperature of my blood rising. I feel like Yellowstone National Park – simmering and steaming on the surface, but with a giant caldera under the surface that could blow and destroy everything. The way I feel I don't need be out in bars. Because if someone went out of their way to look for trouble, they'd fucking find it.

WEDNESDAY 29 NOVEMBER
MIDNIGHT

Struggling; living off practically no sleep. I'm barely eating; or talking to anyone. Cancelled the lads' night out; sick of being skint.

I hate it
I hate myself
I hate my job
I hate my situation
I hate myself

THURSDAY 30 NOVEMBER
8.30PM

I worked thirty minutes late to help someone out. It was good to do something for someone. But those thirty minutes were excruciating.

My mental health is okay. But I'm feeling so negative - dark and dejected. It sometimes gets to all of us doesn't it? When we've just had a gut-full of it all...

At least we'll hopefully do some family stuff this weekend. We're pot-less; but together. I feel like I'm going to put myself through one of our dividing walls.

Rob,

Thanks for so many things. For offering support and advice during a year or so when I was very unwell. And having the understanding to know when I was struggling and to try and help me. Or at least stay in touch with me when I went through a stage of just withdrawing from society altogether. Even though you've battled many challenges yourself, you only ever wanted to help me. You were an immense help so thanks mate, sincerely. Thanks to you and Dan for also making such a huge contribution to this book. The insight you provided shows even within a relatively small group of friends, how common mental illness is.

Thank you mate, for everything,

Steve x

My Invisible World

A group of two or a heaving crowd
The voices inside are always as loud,
As voices drop, people turn around
My mind suffocated by familiar clouds,

What had I said? What had I done?
Totally frozen but wanting to run
My heart beating fast, sweat on my face,
I'd kill to be in anywhere, a different place

As I close my eyes and the mania recedes
My head still pounding again I concede,

Those people didn't even know I was there
Even less about me did they even care,

What did they think? How must I appear?
My actions, their impressions, amongst my fears,

As I walk away my head still bursting
I'm angry, sad, tormented and cursing,

The alternative world that I live every day
Affecting every interaction in every way,

But the hardest thing to accept by far
Is it's part of my being, my paranoia

THIRTEEN. OLD PROBLEMS, NEW HORIZONS

I'm so relieved. Seems the nursery incident was a one off. She hasn't said anything and is still happy to go - still enjoying it. When I picked her up lots of the children waved and said *Bye, Bye*. It was lovely; and for now, eased my anxiety and paranoia. Anxious she was becoming isolated. Paranoid she had no friends. Totally irrational - makes me feel sick. I wish she had a stable dad.

Bubba is poorly again. It's nearly two o'clock and she's woken up three times already... I'm going to run myself into the ground; again. But there's no option when you're a parent.

SATURDAY 2 DECEMBER

10.00PM

Had a lovely day at home just chilling out... Everyone is over-excited about Christmas. Every morning 'advent calendar' time is a huge event - which normally ends in big chocolatey kisses!

Attempting Christmas stuff; but I've no motivation or

interest. It's been a problem for a few days. I ran out of my medication last week... No coincidence the gremlins are creeping back in.

I'm angry; bitter and frustrated. Not so much that I have all these problems and conditions. It's more how I've treated people and how they must view me. Sometimes when you're so deeply entrenched in everything, you just don't see the big picture:

We think too small, like a frog at the bottom of the well. He thinks the sky is only as big as the top of the well. If he surfaced, he could have an entirely different view.

~Mao Tse-Tung~

I still think why me? You might be feeling the same. Why us? What did we do to deserve it? The answer is nothing. So much of our pain and conditions are a result of, or triggered by, other people's behaviour or actions. It's not fair is it? But we must be strong, hold our heads high and be proud of who we are.

I must stick to my routines. And restart my medication as soon as possible.

Rum o'clock...

SUNDAY 3 DECEMBER
8.34PM

The escapism didn't last long. It might have been a few hours of bliss; but the aftermath? It's far from bliss. Headaches are dirty and heavy.

It won't be long until my eldest starts asking questions. Or noticing; if she hasn't already… I mean about the hangovers. Or if I stink of stale booze.

Today we did a Christmas fair. Signs the main event is approaching; and that my calendar is getting busier by the week. I hate it. It's compressing my head, and my patience.

Clock watching at work… Again.

It's early evening and I'm clock watching for a different reason. How many hours sleep will I get? How many hours 'til I leave for work? How many hours until I'm at work? It's dark and depressing.

I need a break from this - from clock watching; myself; everything…

MONDAY 4 DECEMBER
10.17PM

By far the worst day I've had since I finished therapy. Think I only spoke a couple of words all day - just felt totally disconnected.

From my job; my colleagues, my family, myself - from life…

It makes you feel so low. You know people can see you're struggling but you don't care. I'm well past hiding, remember? We should all be past it. We should never smile just because we feel we should. That would indicate we feel ashamed or think we should hide how we feel… Wrong; totally the opposite. The time for bottling stuff up has passed.

The girls were ratty when I got home. We need a good night; desperately. We're all on the edge - you can feel it. Nobody's fault; but makes no difference... I've no idea what I need.

TUESDAY 5 DECEMBER
11.11PM

The spiral... Down, down I go. On the slide; I'm clinging on; barely. Lactic acid burning my hands; my knuckles white, fingertips throbbing...

Medication starting again - it's a big part of my routine and wellbeing. It's also so important to everyone around me. I can't get well and stay well if I'm not looking after myself.

Work is not helping. I just cannot maintain any level of interest. I have good and bad days; but more bad ones... And too many ups and downs during a day. I shouldn't be so unstable. I'm hoping medication and fun, family weekends will be the tonic. I can't even contemplate therapy again. I hate feeling like a perpetual failure.

WEDNESDAY 6 DECEMBER
EARLY

It's five in the morning - been up with our eldest since four. Since ten o'clock last night we've had five wake-ups and hardly any sleep. I have a massive headache; very tight chest; two sick children.

And a sick head...

I'm finding this very difficult to cope with. When I start feeling unwell my thoughts and writing becomes almost all about me. I become so insular and isolated. I'm still learning about managing and coping mechanisms. I don't use people around me enough. Even after everything I've been through. I'm sure you've noticed this too. Maybe you've noticed this within yourself...

But at least we had something to look forward to.... Our eldest's first nativity play...

8.00PM

She was a snowflake!

One of my proudest ever moments... If you've been through this, I imagine you're smiling right now. My heart felt like it was going to burst through my chest. I felt ten feet tall.

She looked so grown up - so beautiful; so incredible. The snowflakes had their own little song and dance. She did so well. Every time she looked up I waved and blew kisses. At the end they all stood together and sang 'Merry Christmas' –

To rapturous applause.

10.05PM

For two hours Bubba hasn't settled so I thought I'd try everything. Changed her sleeping bag to a slightly bigger one... Calpol. Fresh warm milk... And changed her nappy... Bingo! It was full... I felt so guilty. How long had she been like that? Why didn't I check earlier? No wonder she couldn't settle. How would you like trying to sleep with full, soiled pants? I feel so bad. I should've checked earlier. I just want to scream the fucking walls down. Or rip a door off its hinges. My head is screaming inside a silent body.

She's been down for about ten minutes now.

I might even try getting some kip soon.

Once I stop punishing myself.

And the mania recedes...

THURSDAY 7 DECEMBER
5.40PM

A bit better night for Bubba at least... Me? I sat in the living room; staring into nothing. Couldn't control the mania and guilt - couldn't sleep; wide awake for hours.

I finally drifted off, and surprise, surprise, the dreams are back; but with a difference. The usual scenario is meeting a woman. And not being able to close the deal.

This time I did though... Then left the house and deliberately walked in front of a car. I woke up on impact. I hate the idea dreams represent my subconscious mind - reminds me that the suicide stuff is still in there somewhere. That on some level and in some amount, however small; it's always there.

FRIDAY 8 DECEMBER
9.00PM

The house is a cloud of germs. There's a darker cloud forming over me. It's building...

SATURDAY 9 DECEMBER
3.00A.M (TECHNICALLY SUNDAY MORNING.)

Things are strained. Bubba hasn't slept. We've been up all night.

The day started well. An impromptu visit to Dad's; then off for a family snow-globe experience. The snow was shredded biodegradable carrier bags. Weird, but it works. But from then on, it's been hard. My wife and our eldest are getting this flu-thing. Bubba's teething - and been crying for about thirty-six hours.

I'm not well. Physically my chest and breathing are bad, and my mental health is worsening. I've started crying again - for no reason; just randomly. It's not good. I've told my wife, I had no choice.

SUNDAY 10 DECEMBER
8.09PM

Today's been draining. I feel like I'm sinking. The house feels like it's starting to buckle under the weight; under the stress; under the pressure.

Or maybe it's just me?

MONDAY 11 DECEMBER
9.00PM

Running on no sleep finally caught up with me. Mum picked me up. On the way back, I said I'd offered my sister the baby crib, but she didn't want it. I forgot my sister didn't know Mum had told me.

I zoned out; I'm not having it anymore - treading on eggshells just to make other people happy. All it does is make me unhappy and unwell. Why should we sacrifice ourselves? How unwell do we need to make ourselves for the benefit of, or to protect others?

Text to my wife...

My job is depressing me. I think it's one of the main reasons I'm struggling. I'm sorry to burden you. But I need to speak to you more about my problems. Rather than just shutting you out. Trying to protect you doesn't help. Which is what I was doing for years x

Text to Mum...

It's about looking after me too; which for the best part of twenty years I never did. I always put other people first - tried to make them happy - and did myself so much damage. I can't do that anymore. I'm sorry x

I can feel my head starting to suffocate. Life is never simple is it? But you'd hope it's not always this hard.

The dreams are back and this time it's the old one. Meeting a woman and not being able to 'seal the deal'. At least the one in which I get murdered isn't back yet. Waking up with palpitations isn't nice. But at least in that dream I'm not a failure.

At least I have my three ladies. And as Christmas edges nearer, the illnesses seem to be going... After a week of no real sleep the last two nights have been better. Our morning advent calendar ritual is becoming more excitable by the day. And the numbers of sleeps 'til Christmas countdown is on!

But in my other life – the nice guy I swim with realised how little I'm connected to the people around me, and said I was a bit of a loner. I suppose you can only base opinions on the evidence before you, right? I wasn't offended. To be honest it's far less complicated that way. And means I'm not exposing my fragility and paranoia; and making my work life more difficult.

It's crazy to think how someone can be so totally different. It's like the person I am at work isn't really me. It's just a persona I take on for half of my life. It's scary looking at it like that. It's a totally split personality.

Last two nights I've been on the sofa, so my wife can recuperate. Thought the girls would've been waking up due to the coughs - nope; slept through. So, I decided to go back to the bedroom. The last two hours Bubba has been unsettled and crying - unbelievable. I had the hump; banging stuff about, swearing; acting like an idiot basically. I just get like it sometimes - mainly at night; always because of sleep deprivation. It's not on, I know that. But I struggle to control myself. I'm no danger to anyone but me. But it can't be nice to be around. It's horrible to think about yourself in this light. But if you're not honest you'll never get anywhere.

I just want some time with my ladies - proper quality time. Memories stuff. They're both at such wonderful ages. I want to miss as little as possible. Each day is precious. Bedtime is the time of the day I want to stay in forever.

THURSDAY 14 DECEMBER
9.00PM

I've just basically coasted today. Just felt empty. You know the feeling? It's crap, isn't it? Walking round reacting to nothing, having no opinion, because you don't feel anything...

I've told a few people at work I've been feeling unwell. At least they know why I'm quiet and withdrawn. I don't care what people think. But common decency, courtesy and respect cost nothing.

FRIDAY 15 DECEMBER
11.11PM

Family days are now just about Christmas. The days I'm not at work it feels relentless. The amount of energy our eldest has is staggering. But it's the first Christmas she's really understanding and appreciating everything so she's going to be wired, isn't she? And anyway, shouldn't I be enjoying this?

Bubba's crawling so quickly now. Her talking is starting to develop too. And she can answer basic questions - either by nodding her head or saying 'Yeeaahhh'. It's so cute. She can also stand under her own weight. She'll be walking soon; then all hell will break loose.

Our eldest is staying at my parents - we're meeting for breakfast tomorrow before we see Santa. The house is so empty without her. My other two ladies went to bed early. Leaving me in familiar loneliness.

We moan when our houses are mental. But we're bereft and lost when it isn't.

SATURDAY 16 DECEMBER
9.00PM

Breakfast was beautiful family chaos. The poor couple next to us however, who'd clearly rocked up for a quiet Saturday morning breakfast didn't get one... If it were me? I'd have been annoyed and may well have moved table. We were loud and took up loads of space. We were more rock concert than breakfast table.

Think we were all feeling Christmassy. Even though I've not stopped worrying about money for the last two months...

Santa was great. Our eldest really enjoyed speaking to him and his Elf. They also let Bubba get amongst it too! We got some great photos and had a lovely time.

I'm feeling frazzled. Suffering physically which is affecting me mentally. I've been darker - more serious; less happy...

SUNDAY 17 DECEMBER
10.00PM

Today was a hangover day. We were all tired and achy. Illnesses are starting to rear themselves again. My wife's cough is worse. Our eldest has broken out in a bad rash. It makes me cry when I look at her. It's not fair. I can't stand having no control. And if you can't stop getting wound up about things you can't change, and like me, let this stuff really get you down, I feel your anguish and pain. I understand.

You can hear the house and the family creaking. Things are hard. I've been struggling for a few days. Work fills me with dread. Not checked my bank balance for weeks. I'd rather not know how bad things are.

I'm alone.

Time is passing. Tick follows tock follows tick follows tock follows tick. Work moves ever closer. Happiness and relaxation are being replaced by anxiety and trepidation.

Being so deeply affected by something I can't control.

MONDAY 18 DECEMBER
10.00PM

My life… At least at work, is just an existence. I'm a robot; it feels like what's left of my soul is disintegrating.

The house is very poorly. It's simply awful timing. Back to broken nights, tears and strained emotions. Well me anyway. My wife's cough is so bad. She's in our bed; and me? I'm on the living room sofa with Bubba's monitor next to me. She's sleeping soundly for now… That makes one of us.

TUESDAY 19 DECEMBER
9.00PM

Got to the station and my wife messaged me. She's very poorly, so I had to go home. When I did she went straight to bed.

Using your holiday to look after your family means even less 'me time' and will affect my mental health somewhere down the line.

I'm not even bothered about how selfish I'm feeling. I've no filter. And can't control the way I'm feeling even if I wanted to.

I'm strung out. This is when having a young family is so tough. It's not their fault, your children, when things are so strained is it? They need you. They have nobody else. What you need, well sometimes it's just not important. And you can't get it anyway.

WEDNESDAY 20 DECEMBER
10.00PM

Bad night leading to bad day - I'm buckling.

Surely, you've had these days? When you just want to shut the door... Sit down and say, 'no more'? Everything is hard work. Trying to look after your family – trying to look after yourself...

The house is quiet... Even my mind aches. Writing is hard. For anyone who thinks this is therapeutic, and for my own benefit, if that was the case there'd be gaps of days and even weeks from the start until now.

But I've kept going... Because it's real life; showing my faults and insecurities... And baring my soul – it's the only way this will work. Showing what people who are suffering in silence might be going through as I write, and as you read. Wherever in the world you're reading this, no matter how far away from me, we're in this together. You're not, and will never be, alone.

THURSDAY 21 DECEMBER
10.00PM

Three days in a row. I've had enough… Christmas gets closer… But nobody is feeling festive.

It's so selfish; but I need some time away from the house; my family. I'm trying not to get paranoid and over-analyse what you might be thinking about this, about me. How can he say stuff like that? He's so selfish! I'd never be like that. Maybe you wouldn't? Maybe you'd just think some of this stuff, but never say it… Say what you want, I'm being honest.

I've said throughout that I'll accept people, and you, judging me.

But how many people go through emotions like this but just bottle them up? And how much damage is that doing? Not just to them, but the people they love, the people closest to them?

FRIDAY 22 DECEMBER
10.57PM

Officially the first day of my Christmas holiday… Wouldn't know it though… I feel about as festive as a turkey that's just been looked at by Bernard Matthews (*vegetarian analogies are available*).

Our eldest is going to my parents' house tonight. But she's fine; it's Bubba who is so exhausting. She just won't sleep and is coughing all the time. I think I've aged a year in a month.

Self-medication has hit the skids. Hopefully we'll be well enough to visit Santa tomorrow.

Hoping my wife and I can try and get some quality time together.

Currently…? Absolutely no chance…

SATURDAY 23 DECEMBER
IT'S SO LATE… TIME IS LOSING MEANING

Had a manic family breakfast in a local pub chain… Again, we disturbed everyone around us. I get so paranoid in these situations. And end up apologising and over-compensating. Normally it's the self-deprecation default. You can get away with most things this way.

Nanny and Grandad came to see Santa with us. It grates on me that because of modern day society children can't sit on Santa's lap anymore. How is standing next to him the same? It's not…

CHRISTMAS EVE
(WELL IT'S 3.00AM, SO CHRISTMAS DAY)

Another lovely Christmas adventure - we'd pre-booked tickets to see (another) Santa at the light railway in Romney. We've had to make up so many stories about Santa's helpers and his elves. We're currently seeing Santa every few days… And he looks different every time!

We also found a score (twenty quid) in the car park. I felt guilty about keeping it but there were no cars around us, so I couldn't ask anyone anyway. And my wife said I've lost enough money in the past which is true. I'm often absent minded and notoriously useless.

Bubba was so ill, screaming the house down. So about two hours ago I took her for a walk along by the lakes. It's just another example of the crazy things you do as a parent. You'll do anything to help them feel better; however ludicrous the remedy.

CHRISTMAS DAY

(2.00AM, TECHNICALLY IT'S ALREADY OVER)

There was paper everywhere today. And Bubba was everywhere! My wife got me loads. What I got her was embarrassing by comparison. And the replacement locket necklace didn't even fit. But the girls loved their presents.

Breakfast with my parents was lovely. But everyone apart from me was ill.

It was calmer at my mother-in-law's. She mentioned that she saw me this morning when she was driving home from mass. I forgot I was only wearing sandals, shorts and t-shirt.

By early evening everyone was stuffed and tired. We got home; finally put our feet up... And then it started. Violent stomach upset, through the eye of a needle stuff... Been up and down to the toilet for hours... Merry Christmas!

Sincerely though - I wish you all fun, family-time, happiness and love x

Text to my wife…

I'm sorry I'm so useless. And that I'm spoiling Christmas. Hopefully I'll be better tomorrow. I'm feeling rough. But stomach a little better x

BOXING DAY
9.00PM

The relentless illness is seriously bringing me down. I've not been self-medicating for about a week. Not for asthma; my throat; my head. I'm struggling to cope. November and December have been very difficult.

Boxing Day was always my nan's day. A big lunch and all her families around her… Filling her house with love and laughter – today feels empty. I didn't think it would affect me; but I was wrong. She was such a sweet, lovely lady. I miss you, Nan x

I've got my appointments early doors tomorrow. I'm a little worried about the abdominal scan. Well wouldn't you be? Not sure what my asthma nurse is going to say. It's been bad for a while.

This house is a mess.

I'm a mess.

You know if you've been in this position how it goes... And that's downhill. My eldest has given her skin infection to me. My wife's still not great - back and shoulder, and this chest infection. My mental illness is affecting our relationship again - what I really mean is I've been an arsehole. Being honest is hard. It's not nice. But it's my fault.

Abdominal scan earlier... Looks like things are all okay.

The appointment with my asthma specialist was pointless because I was unwell; none of the chest capacity figures were accurate. I need to rebook, again. It's just one thing after another. I'm failing in every aspect of my life - as a husband and father; son and employee - and my health.

I honestly think it's been weeks since I was happy. Since I smiled because I really wanted to...

I call it the *uncontrollable smile.*

Text to my wife...

You haven't pissed me off. I've just been making sure she has been medicated, however she has seemed, every night for the last week. And that's been broken. Honestly? It's my first boxing day without any grandparents. It's weird and not nice. Secondly, I've had no time to recover because I've been frequently agitated. Now I'm overtired, grumpy and hungry. But everyone has been ill. And I've had no chance to talk about them. Because I've been flat out trying to look after everyone else; so that's honestly where I am. I'm going to go for a coffee tomorrow after the doctor and try to clear

my head a bit, because currently it's not great. But that my issue.
And not your fault x

THURSDAY 28 DECEMBER
11.00PM

One of my close friends who has suffered from mental illness is worried about me. He's asked me to go to my doctor and discuss pharmaceutical medication/treatment. I haven't replied. I'm not admitting defeat just yet. This is absolutely no disrespect to anyone taking them. I've already said these drugs save lives. But I just can't bear the thought of taking them.

FRIDAY 29 DECEMBER
11.30PM

I can't shave because of this skin infection. It's taken away what little self-esteem and confidence I had left. Bubba isn't sleeping, she's so poorly. And my wife probably needs a holiday and a break from me. She even said it's been a difficult Christmas. And it's not like her to say things like that. I don't blame her though... She's right.

Pressure isn't nice is it? And sometimes it's difficult to find a release isn't it? Ever felt like you just want to literally tear your hair out? I think feeling that pain, inflicting that pain, might help release some of the pressure. I want to scream until my throat is sore. But where can you without attracting unwanted attention... You can't... I just want to shred my skin off with my bare hands.

SATURDAY 30 DECEMBER
10.30PM

I'm already getting anxious about going back to work.

It's meaning I don't get to spend any quality time with my wife either. Her physical health hasn't been great. And our body clocks are totally out of sync. I get home from work. And she's ready for bed. I get an hour with the girls. Then they're in bed. And I'm left on my own. Evenings are lonely. It was when I was like this, and living in Maidstone, I was drinking every night of the week. But at least that's not going to happen again.

SUNDAY 31 DECEMBER
9.00PM - THE FINAL ENTRY

Text to Mum....

Thank you for the shopping. Sorry, I'm not myself at the moment. The last two weeks have been so stressful. I had to cancel seeing my mates over Christmas. And I've barely left the house. I hope you have a lovely time. Don't worry about me. I'll muddle through x

For the second year in a row, I'm sitting alone in my living room on New Years' Eve drinking bubbly stuff. Everyone has long gone to bed. It's no fun but best for everyone. I'm going over the last year and it's bending my head. So much has happened. Why don't you do the same......?

- What's made you happy?
- What has made you sad/angry/depressed/frustrated?
- Did you process all the crap, and talk about how you felt?
- Do you know what your main stress triggers are?
- Can you feel when they're starting to affect you?
- Do you have coping mechanisms? And do they work?
- Have you used them before? If they involve drugs/alcohol, are you in control of the usage?
- Have you ever asked anyone for help?
- Have you thought about how your behaviour has impacted on other people?
- Have you talked about how other people's behaviour has impacted on you?
- Or have you just bottled everything up?
- Are you happy in your home/work/social life? If not, think about making changes. Never just settle; you're better and more important than that.
- Are you still trying to achieve your dreams and aspirations? Or have you given up on them? If so why? What barriers are impossible to overcome...? None!
- And finally, are you the person you want to be? Are you

happy when you look in the mirror? And I mean when you really look...

This year, and this book has been hard. It's not nice being on show, so vulnerable, so open. I've made some progress. But lapsed too - and badly; and publicly. But I've always wanted this to be real. And often there's no quick fix. No happily ever after. Life is beautiful and amazing. But it can be difficult and painful. My mental illness isn't good going into 2018. But I'm optimistic I can make changes, be strong; manage my demons. And enjoy my life.

Like everything in life. You get out what you put in. To help yourself you must be ready. And know what you want to achieve. Otherwise you'll end up wasting your time and feeling worse. But if the timing is right, therapy can be a life changing experience. The most important thing is, to take your time and make the right decisions for you; not those around you.

Opening-up to people is one of the hardest things I have ever done. It made me feel like a worthless, embarrassing excuse for a human being. Over the last year I've hurt, infuriated, shocked, angered and surprised people. And yes, the truth hurts, absolutely. But what I discovered is that by dropping the macho façade and letting people in and sharing stuff with them, you can make relationships even stronger.

I found that for the first time in my life people started to get to know me. And although I hated being so vulnerable, people who truly care about you only care that you're well, safe and happy.

I'm still bottling some stuff up, holding back. But you can't unload everything at once... I still haven't told my parents, but I will before they read this... If you've ever battled any of the conditions I've spoken about, I'm appealing to you. Swallow your pride (it's overrated, trust me). Take the first step, love yourself...

Talking changes lives...

Once you start to understand and love yourself, you'll be able to love other people and let them love you. Good luck and good health.

Happy living... Enjoy life x

My blonde bombshell

At a time of my life I was totally lost
Didn't value my life, didn't give a toss

Walking through town, totally dejected
Even after a night when I wasn't rejected,

Stumbling towards the next boozy bar
I spotted a gorgeous blonde from afar

We then talked among friends, planning a drink,
Of this amazing woman I could only think

Tried to chill out, tried to look cool
And not look like an absolute fool

Out of my league, but that was fine
My idea wasn't charm, but dry white wine!

Forget Cupid's arrow, the love bug had bitten,
From the very first minute, totally smitten

From that day on the love of my life,
I dreamed you'd become my darling wife

And now we have two beautiful girls,
Three wonderful ladies who are my world

No words can describe how amazing she is;
So, all I could do was attempt to do this.

I love you sweetheart.
Thank you for sticking by me x

FOURTEEN. A PAINFUL RETURN –
POST-NATAL/POSTPARTUM DEPRESSION

1ST MAY 2018

I'd planned not to do any writing after New Year's Eve. But this can't be ignored. It's not a surprise that I'm back in therapy. It's part of the illness, and part of recovery. But what is a surprise, and not a nice one, is why.

(I'd also planned to leave this chapter heading out of the contents page and leave it as a surprise. The reason? To signify how I and so many of us, suffer in silence, and often don't talk until the end, when things get really, very bad. But I had to conform to book writing convention and include it.)

For a while I've been having thoughts about harming our children - which I've **never** done. And **never** will do. But how this has manifested itself is in me self-harming… Things like picking up boiling kettles and saucepans by the main part, not the handles and walking on hot surfaces barefoot (for example, last week I walked a mile along a pavement in the hottest part of the day while with my daughters in their buggy, it was agony). I also stubbed cigarettes out on myself (I'm a non-smoker).

These, according to my therapist are common symptoms of postnatal depression.

This illness has not been extensively researched and we really don't know too much about the size of the problem, particularly among men. I think because it's even more embarrassing than having to admit other types of mental health issues. For me personally, the shame is so much greater.

This needs to be clear. I consider myself a kind, caring person. A loving husband and devoted, (over) protective dad. These feelings and visions I started to experience made me feel physically sick, made me despise myself. I was, and am, disgusted with myself and hate myself. That's why I self-harmed; to try and get rid of those feelings.

I struggle to deal with the fact I can't control when one of these thoughts will pollute my head - which is why I'm self-harming. I feel it's what I deserve (to be punished for having such disgusting and shameful thoughts).

This is the worst thing I've ever experienced. When I told my wife; she broke down. And I can't blame her, not for a second. Ultimately people need to trust you're in control and getting the help you need. But, as I explained, I only have these feelings at night, when wake-ups are frequent and sleep in short supply.

But it's at these times I overcompensate. By cuddling and holding my girls a little longer and a little tighter. So, the vibes and energy they feel from me are full of love. Not the same care I'm taking of myself. But that's a separate issue.

But however painful honesty is in the short term. It's nothing compared to how bad things could get if you suffer in silence. I know. Even in the few weeks I kept this to myself I went downhill so fast; it was scary. And you must stop it as soon as you can. Honesty can (re)build trust, hope and strengthen relationships.

To offer some balance I've also done some reading about this. The NCT has a website with a lot of excellent information about symptoms, and support. Their research also found *More than 1 in 3 new fathers (38%) are concerned about their mental health. In general, studies have shown that one in 10 dads has PND and fathers also appear to be more likely to suffer from depression three to six months after their baby is born.* You can find more information at the NCT (National Childbirth Trust) website. This quote is from a press release about fathers and mental health.

There are so many charities doing amazing work. Mind has an excellent website where you can find great information. As well as people who have shared their experiences.

If you are experiencing any symptoms related to PND please talk to your doctor. There is a combination of excellent professional help, and local focus groups where you can share your experiences and not feel alone anymore.

I'm hoping therapy will continue to help. Not just me, but everyone currently going through this, and the family and friends who love and support them.

The reality? This is going to take longer than I ever thought to make progress.

I'm only just starting to understand how bad things are. But I don't want to end with negativity… With knowledge and understanding comes control. And I truly believe that we can overcome anything.

And together we will x

Good luck; and good mental health x

Steve x